THE GREAT
BOOK OF SPAIN

Interesting Stories, Spanish History
& Random Facts About Spain

History & Fun Facts Volume 3

BILL O'NEILL

ISBN: 978-1-64845-048-8

DON'T FORGET YOUR
FREE BOOKS

CONTENTS

CHAPTER TWO:
SPAIN'S MODERN HISTORY 37

CHAPTER THREE:
SPAIN'S GEOGRAPHY, CLIMATE, AND
INDUSTRY...71

CHAPTER SIX:
WEIRD SPAIN—LEGENDS, GHOST STORIES,
AND THE STRANGE! 151

INTRODUCTION

What do you really know about Spain?

You probably know that Spain is a European country and that the people there speak Spanish. You may also know that it is on the Mediterranean Sea and that it has some pretty nice beaches.

But that is only a very small part of Spain's story.

This book will explore all of the topics that have made Spain an important and interesting country for several centuries. You will learn about Spain's history, geography, economy, and so much more in this book that is part tour guide and 100% fun!

This book is broken up into six easy-to-follow chapters with 13 to 15 short stories in each that will help you learn more about Spain. At the end of each chapter, we'll ask some trivia questions to find out how much attention you've been paying.

You will be introduced to every aspect of Spain in a way that is exciting and engaging. Follow along as you witness Spain's development from a Roman province to being part of the European Union. Along the way, you'll learn about the country's vibrant film industry, history of artists, and its love of sports.

This book will also answer some of the following questions:

- How did Hannibal get his start in Spain?
- What was the Reconquista?
- When was the Spanish Civil War?
- How did some Spanish film stars become international icons?
- What are the most popular sports in Spain?
- Who were some of Spain's best artists and writers?
- Were Don Juan and El Cid real people?
- Where are the Pillars of Hercules?
- Where is Spain's premier party spot?
- What's the deal with siestas?

And so much more!

Let's get started, shall we?

CHAPTER ONE:

SPAIN'S EARLY HISTORY

Spain's location on the shores of the Mediterranean Sea has guaranteed that it played a major role in the world's geopolitical struggles throughout history. There have been so many important events and people that given Spain prominence throughout history that we have to break the country's history into two chapters! In this chapter, we'll look at Spain's history from the Paleolithic Period until about 1,500 CE.

I know what you're thinking: "Man, that's a lot of time to cover!"

Yes, you're right, so buckle in for an incredible historical ride. And I guarantee it will be an exciting adventure.

We'll explore incredible cave paintings, examine how a people known as the Iberians ruled most of Spain, and ultimately, how the country got its name. We'll also meet Hannibal and the Carthaginians and discuss how Rome came to rule Spain. Then we'll meet a bunch of different people who ruled Spain but had names that sounded more like biker gangs: the Vandals, the Sueves, and the Visigoths.

Did you know that Spain was a Muslim-dominated country for several centuries? That's another interesting historical fact we'll explore, along with how the Muslims were eventually driven out of the land.

So Easy a Caveman Could Do It?

There is often the idea that the humans of the Paleolithic Era (Old Stone Age), which lasted until about 10,000 years ago, were little more than dumb brutes. If anything, though, the opposite was true. Paleolithic humans invented numerous tools for hunting, cooking, and making skins from scratch.

They also made some incredible art!

You may have read about the cave paintings from Lascaux, France. Not far to the southwest, over the border in Spain, is another, equally impressive site, known as the Cave of Altamira.

The cave was discovered in the late 19th century by a couple of Spanish archeologists and was dated to about 36,000 years ago. Subsequent studies have revealed that humans lived in the mouth of the more than 3,000-foot long cave but left their art on the walls and ceiling throughout. Like in the Lascaux Cave, the paintings in the Cave of Altamira depict bison and other animals the Paleolithic inhabitants hunted.

The paintings were made from charcoal, ochre, and hematite and show an incredibly advanced technique and talent: many of the animals are shaded and show perspective, which was an artistic technique not used commonly until thousands of years later. The technique of the paintings was so advanced that many thought they were done in modern times. Recent carbon dating has proved that they are prehistoric in origin.

The Cave of Altamira isn't the only cave of its type in Spain. Several other similar, yet smaller, caves are also located in northern Spain around the Pyrenees Mountains.

Spain's Ancient Tombs

After 10,000 BCE, the first signs of the Neolithic Period (New Stone Age) began in the Fertile Crescent of the Middle East and Egypt. The people in these regions learned to farm and how to domesticate animals, eventually spreading those concepts to other places. The idea of farming entered Europe via Greece around 6,500 BCE and quickly spread around the Mediterranean Basin, reaching what is today Spain by 6,000 BCE. By 5,000 BCE, most of the coastal areas of Spain were being farmed and most of the prerequisites of what western academics define as "civilization" had been met.

The most impressive aspect of Neolithic Spain, however, were the countless megaliths that were built in these coastal areas.

The term "megalith" simply denotes a large stone structure. In the case of Neolithic Spain, they were dolmen burial chambers constructed in post and lintel form. Los Millares, Romeral, and El Barranquete on the south Mediterranean coast of Spain are home to several of these impressive structures, but more can be found along the Atlantic coast and on both sides of the Pyrenees. The people who created these monuments were of a similar prehistoric culture to those that erected Stonehenge in England—they may have even originated in Spain.

Later in the Neolithic Period, after 2,500 BCE, another Neolithic culture developed in Spain known as the "Bell Beaker" culture. It was named for the pottery associated with it, which look like upside-down bells. Bell Beakers spread from Spain to central Europe, but their dominance in Europe was short-lived.

Spain and Europe were about to be radically changed by the Bronze Age.

The Bronze Age Comes to Spain

The Bronze Age was a period when great changes in technology and society occurred and when empires rose and fell. In the Ancient Near East (corresponding roughly to the Modern Middle East), the Bronze Age began in about 3,300 BCE and lasted until around 1,200 BCE, while in Europe it took place a little later and lasted a little longer.

In what would become Spain, the Bronze Age began around 1,800 BCE.

There were two different cultures in Bronze Age Spain. Northern Spain was part of the "Urnfield Culture" that was dominant in much of central Europe during the Bronze Age. It was called the "Urnfield Culture" because individuals were cremated and their remains were placed in urns before being interred in large cemeteries or urnfields. The Urnfield Culture's elites' remains were interred in tumuli (burial mounds) with their possessions.

Although southern and western Spain were separate from the Urnfield Culture, they too were in the Bronze Age at the same time, with modern archaeological work yielding some impressive finds from certain locations.

A fortified site was built at El Argar on the Mediterranean coast, which was able to influence much of southern Spain. Although these Bronze Age

Spaniards did not yet have writing, their metallurgical and other building skills were quite advanced. A shipwreck dated to the Late Bronze Age was discovered in 1923 near the southern Atlantic coastal town of Huelva. The wreck is significant because it contained 200 bronze weapons, indicating that warfare and territorial expansion were a part of Bronze Age Spain.

However, by 750 BCE, the idea of ironworking had come to Spain, ushering in the Iron Age and an era during which Spain would begin to acquire its current ethnic and cultural identity.

Celts and Iberians

The Iron Age meant big changes for Europe generally and Spain in particular. Tribes of Indo-Europeans, who are the ancestors of modern Europeans, began populating the continent and either mixing with or driving out the pre-Indo-European peoples.

By 500 BCE the Celts were the dominant people in central and western Europe, which included northern and western Spain.

The warlike Celts conquered and mixed with the native people of Spain—the Iberians—southwest of the Pyrenees but left them alone for the most part along the Mediterranean coast.

The Iberians were a mining and merchant people,

who developed trade ties with both the Phoenicians and Greeks. The Iberian language is yet to be deciphered, so their name actually comes from the word the Greeks used to refer to them and their land.

The term "Iberian" stuck through ancient, medieval, and modern times and Iberia is still used to refer to Portugal and Spain collectively—the Iberian peninsulas.

The Iberians developed sophisticated art and architecture, built important cities such as Gades (modern Cadiz), and developed writing by 500 BCE.

One thing the Iberians weren't good at was warfare, which was needed in their neighborhood. You see, by the 5th century BCE, the Mediterranean was a playground for the powerful—and the powerful were the ones with the biggest armies and navies.

And the Iberians were late to the party on military building.

A New Player Emerges

As the Iberians were quietly building an advanced society in southern Spain, the Phoenicians were colonizing the western Mediterranean. One colony, in particular, became especially powerful—Carthage.

Carthage was founded by Phoenician settlers from

Tyre in either the 8th or 7th centuries BCE. By 573 BCE, it had become independent and not long after, its rulers set their sights on building an empire. Located on the coast of what is today Tunisia, Carthage captured Sardinia and most of the other western Mediterranean islands and the southern Iberian coast by the early 3rd century BCE.

Gades became a Carthaginian city and later other Carthaginian cities, such as Carthago Novo (New Carthage), were built on Spain's Mediterranean coastline.

But not everyone was happy with the situation.

The Romans were also building an empire in the western Mediterranean, so in 264 BCE the two powers went to war in what is known as the First Punic War (Punic was the language of the Carthaginians). When the war ended in 241 BCE, the Carthaginians lost Sardinia, Corsica, and Sicily, but they later gained more land in Spain.

It would be from Spain that the Carthaginians launched one of the most spectacular military campaigns in world history, led by a man with an unforgettable name, riding animals that are usually associated more with circuses than war.

Here Come the Elephants!

The modern city of Sagunto, Spain is one of the most

significant cities in the ancient world and was the site where an epic war began. In 219 BCE, Saguntum—as it was then called—was a prosperous independent city closely aligned with Rome. Its primarily Iberian-descended people were peaceful merchants, but that all changed when a Carthaginian general named Hannibal came to town.

Hannibal Barca was a tough, crafty, and wily general who wanted to punish the Romans for defeating Carthage in the First Punic War.

And he didn't care who got in his way to achieve that goal.

Hannibal expanded the Carthaginian territory from the Mediterranean coast of Spain inland to the Guadalquivir River, conquering many cities and building a few in the process.

But the people of Saguntum were an obstacle in his way. After laying siege to the city for several months, he finally conquered it amid much bloodshed, which started the Second Punic War (218-202 BCE).

Hannibal assembled a massive army of 50,000 men, 9,000 cavalry, and 37 war elephants—yes, you heard that right, elephants!—and marched into Italy. Although he was never able to take Rome, he occupied southern Italy for more than ten years. The Romans had no answer to Hannibal until a man named Scipio was tasked with defeating him.

Scipio's answer? Bring the war back to Spain!

The Roman general retook Saguntum and prevented Hannibal's brother, Hasdrubal, from leading another army complete with elephants into Italy. The elephants may have had initial shock and awe value, but the Romans quickly got over it and won the war.

The Carthaginians were gone, but Spain was placed under Roman rule for nearly 700 years.

Spain Gets Its Name

The Romans are known today for their military prowess, which was certainly earned, but it's not the complete story. The Roman Republic and the Roman Empire lasted for nearly 1,000 years; longer if you include the Byzantine Empire. Although it is true that the Romans expanded and defended their borders through force, they maintained their state for that long period primarily through diplomacy and trade.

Conquered peoples were incorporated into the empire, and if their land was valuable and the people made efforts to "Romanize," things generally went smoothly.

For Spain, the situation was mostly peaceful, although there was one major period of unrest. We'll get to that soon.

After the Romans defeated the Carthaginians in the Second Punic War, all of Iberia was incorporated into the Roman Republic and given a new name— *Hispania*.

You are probably thinking you've heard that word before, probably referring to Latin American people. Yes, the modern term "Hispanic" is remotely derived from the ancient term. Modern Hispanics primarily speak Spanish or Portuguese, but the original, ancient term was confined to the Iberian Peninsula.

Hispania was originally divided into two provinces—Hispania Citerior (Nearer Spain) and Hispania Ulterior (Further Spain)—with Ulterior being on Spain's southern coast and Citerior being along the coastline to the Pyrenees Mountains. The Romans found the two provinces to be quite lucrative and pliable: they were already mining valuable mineral resources and extensive trade had been taking place there for more than 2,000 years.

The Iberians, Celts, Celtiberians, and Carthaginians who had been living in Spain were accustomed to law, order, and civilization, so they were more than willing to cooperate with their new Roman masters. The favorable political, cultural, and economic conditions in Spain, along with a climate that resembled Rome's, meant that Romans of all classes began flooding the provinces to start over, expand their businesses, or just to get away from the hustle and bustle of Rome.

By the early 1st century BCE, Further and Nearer Spain had grown to encompass all but the northcentral part of the Iberian Peninsula. Everything seemed to be going well for Spain; the people were being incorporated into the Roman Republic and there was plenty of food and coins to go around.

However, the Romans were about to fall out among themselves, often with Spain as their battlefield.

Spain Becomes a Battlefield

The 1st century BCE was an extremely turbulent time in Rome. Class conflict, slave uprisings, and military coups were the order of the day. Yes, this was the period of the legendary Spartacus, but it was also when a Roman general named Sertorius almost led Spain to independence from Rome.

Sertorius was well-liked by all classes and ethnic groups in Spain and was persuaded by many to lead a rebellion against Rome. He accepted, which began the Sertorian War (80-72 BCE) in Spain. Sertorius defeated the Romans in numerous battles before the general Pompey was sent to Spain to reduce his army. Although unable to defeat Sertorius decisively, Pompey had the resources of the Roman Army and so was able to gradually weaken the rebel general's forces.

It was a collection of assassins' knives that finally ended the rebellion though.

With Sertorius gone, Pompey reorganized the Spanish provinces and settled in to enjoy his victory.

But that wasn't the end for Spain in the 1st century.

In 60 BCE, Pompey, Julius Caesar, and Crassus formed the "First Triumvirate," which was a non-legally binding military alliance. The men divided the Roman territory among themselves, with Pompey being given control of Spain. As is so common when there's more than one alpha dog in the room, Pompey and Caesar's relationship eventually soured and the men led their armies against each other.

Caesar won, Pompey was assassinated, and all seemed well for the glorious general.

But Pompey's sons weren't going away quietly.

In 45 BC, Caesar led his army to the plains of Munda in southern Spain to face a numerically superior army led by Pompey's sons. Being outnumbered was never a problem for Caesar, though; he defeated the armies after several hours of heavy fighting.

Less than a year later, Caesar was made "Dictator for Life" of Rome.

But we all know how that ended, right?

For Spain, this marked the end of any major battles or uprisings for more than 300 years. In this era, known as the "Augustan Peace," Spain grew economically and culturally, contributing significantly to the Roman Empire and civilization in general.

Emperors, Philosophers, and Poets Were Born in Spain

When the smoke of the Roman Civil Wars cleared in 30 BCE, Octavian was the winner and became Rome's first emperor, Augustus Caesar. Augustus dedicated plenty of time and resources to making Spain a first-class colony. He divided the entire Iberian Peninsula into three separate provinces: Lusitania in the west, Baetica in the south, and Tarraconensis in the east and north.

State-of-the-art roads were built to connect many of the new cities with the existing ones and aqueducts were also built to bring water to them. Gold, silver, iron, copper, tin, and lead were all mined in Spain, while wheat, wine, and horses became Spain's principal agricultural exports.

By the early 1st century CE, Spain was among

Rome's wealthiest colonies and the standard of living of its people was on a similar level to Italy. As a result, many elite Roman families began moving to Spain, at first part-time, but eventually year-round. Soon, some of Rome's most influential people were being born in Spain.

The emperors Trajan, Hadrian, and Theodosius I were all born in Spain. Trajan was known for his wars in the 1st century CE, while Hadrian is remembered for the wall he built across Britain beginning in 122 CE. Theodosius I is important because he was the last emperor to rule over a unified Roman Empire, from 392-395 CE.

Maybe even more important and impactful on Roman culture, however, were the many writers, scientists, and philosophers who were born in Spain.

The rhetorician Quintilian was born in Calagurris on the Ebro River. Not far from him, Martial the poet was born in Bilbilis. Another famous poet, Prudentius, was born in Tarraconensis sometime in the 5th century CE.

Corduba (modern Cordova) was the home of both Seneca the Elder and Seneca the Younger, who amazed many with their rhetoric and philosophy.

Corduba was also the birthplace of the famous 1st century CE poet, Lucan.

Pomponius Mela, the influential 1st century CE

geographer, was born in Tingentera on the Strait of Gibraltar. Just a few miles up the Atlantic coast—and at about the same time—Columella lived in Gades (modern Cadiz). Columella wrote books about farming and agriculture that were widely read in Rome and later survived the Dark Ages.

So, Spain played a vital role in the Roman Empire, not just in terms of its plentiful natural resources but also due to the brains and leadership of the Spanish people. By the first couple of centuries CE, Spain had come into its own as an important country on the European stage.

Español

Perhaps Spain's greatest contribution to the modern world is its language, Spanish. Spanish is the native language of nearly 500 million people in dozens of countries and ranks number two in the world as the most widely spoken native language, just behind Mandarin Chinese. Besides Spain, it is the primary language throughout most of Latin America and, in addition to the hundreds of millions of native speakers, tens of millions of people around the world know some Spanish.

So how then did Spanish become the language of Spain and so many other countries?

Well, Spanish is in the Indo-European language

family—like English and German, among other languages—and is part of the Romance subfamily along with Latin, French, Portuguese, Italian, and Romanian. The term "Romance" has to do with all of those languages being derived from the language of Rome, Latin, not because they necessarily sound sexy, although some of them do sound pretty nice to English speakers!

Among Spain's early inhabitants, the Iberians spoke a non-Indo-European language and the Celts spoke various dialects of Celtic, which although Indo-European, is in a different subfamily than the Romance languages. The Romans brought Latin to Spain and, as the Spanish colonies developed and the Iberian Peninsula became fully integrated into the Roman Empire, it became the primary language of Spain.

But things change and languages evolve.

As the Roman Empire began to collapse in the 4th century CE, regional Latin dialects began to evolve into distinct yet related languages. For example, the Latin spoken on Rome's northeastern frontier was influenced by the local Slavic languages and became Romanian. Likewise, on the northwestern frontier, Germanic languages influenced Latin, leading to the creation of French.

Spanish evolved similarly, taking influences from

German and then later Arabic.

We'll get to how that happened in a little bit.

Today, "Spanish Spanish"—the kind of Spanish spoken in Spain—is often referred to as "Castilian" or "castellano" for the former Kingdom of Castile in northern Spain, while dialects spoken in countries such as Mexico are called "Español."

All of this began over 2,000 years ago when the Romans brought their government and culture to the Iberian Peninsula.

Vandalizing Spain

The 5th century CE marked the beginning of the end for Rome and also the beginning of the Dark Ages. As Rome came to rely more and more on Germans to staff their military, ironically, it was also Germanic tribes that helped to bring Rome down.

It's not as if Rome didn't have some responsibility for its demise, though.

As the Romans found it increasingly difficult to defeat the almost endless hordes of Germanic tribes making their way into the Empire, they resorted to non-military tactics to achieve their objectives. They often paid ransoms to Germanic warlords or would even give entire tribes official "federated" status. By 409, Spain would suffer under the wrath of these tribes that often had colorful-sounding names but were absolutely ruthless in their use of violence.

In 409 CE, two Germanic tribes—the Vandals and Sueves—and a non-Germanic tribe—the Alans—crossed the Pyrenees into Spain as an allied invading army.

Yes, there was a people called the Vandals, and yes, that is where the modern term "vandalism" originated. After first pillaging and vandalizing their way through Gaul (France), the Vandals led their allies into the rich territory of Spain. The Vandals and their allies quickly established new kingdoms in Spain and thumbed their noses at Rome.

After all, what could the Romans do?

The Romans first tried to make deals with the Vandals, and when that didn't work, they did the only thing they could—they asked an equally ruthless Germanic tribe for assistance.

The Romans called the Visigoths—yes, that was also an actual name of a German tribe—for assistance in 418 CE. The Visigoths and the Vandals turned Spain into a battlefield, leaving death, destruction, and—of course—vandalism wherever they met. Finally, in 429 CE, the Vandals left for North Africa, where they made a new deal with the Romans that allowed them to establish another kingdom.

The Visigoths were given federated status and allowed to rule Spain as they desired.

The era of Germanic tribes with cool names causing mayhem and carnage was over in Spain. The Visigoths established a royal dynasty, left their imprint on the Spanish language, and ushered in an era of peace that would last for nearly another 300 years.

But by now I'm sure you've figured out that 300 years is a long time for Spain to go without a major war.

Muslims Ruled Spain for Hundreds of Years

You probably don't think of Spain as a Muslim country because today it is predominately Roman Catholic. Spain exported these strong Catholic values to Latin America and the Philippines. However, for most of the Middle Ages, most of Spain was ruled by Muslims.

The Visigoths were able to keep the country in relative peace, but their rule was plagued by instability and internal conflicts.

It was obvious that Spain was ripe for the pickings, so it was only a matter of who would answer the call and when.

The "who" was the Berber Muslims of North Africa and the "when" was 711 CE.

The Berbers made the short trip across the Strait of Gibraltar that year and quickly overran southern Spain. By 718 CE, they had conquered most of Spain and were poised to cross the Pyrenees and do the same to Gaul.

But they were stopped by the Frankish leader Charles Martel in 732. After that year, a process began in Spain known as the *Reconquista*, whereby the surviving Christian kingdoms of the north slowly won Spain back from the Muslims. The long-lasting war was marked by extensive periods of peace and sometimes even cooperation among the leaders, but before long extremely bitter warfare would always break out again. The fighting became even more ferocious when Christian Crusader knights began returning from the Middle East in the 12th century CE.

The Reconquista would continue until the end of the 15th century CE.

But we'll get back to that in a while.

Not all aspects of Muslim rule in Spain were violent nor were the relations between Muslims and Christian always acrimonious. Christians were expected to observe Islamic law, but there were no real attempts by the main Islamic government—known as the Caliphate of Cordoba—to convert the native Christians. By 900 CE, Cordoba was the largest city in Europe, and this was largely the result of Arab and Berber immigration from other Islamic caliphates.

The new hybrid culture became known as "Moorish" and the people of Islamic Spain as "Moors." The native Christians adapted to this new reality, eventually adopting elements of Arab and Berber culture into Spanish language, food, clothing, and architecture. This influence is called "Mozarab" and is most apparent in the architecture of medieval southern Spain.

The situation in northern Spain, however, was quite different.

The people there expelled the Muslims pretty early, and therefore, a Moorish culture never developed in the regions and kingdoms of Asturias, Castile, Navarre, Leon, Aragon, and Barcelona.

It was from these places where the native Christians launched their attacks to drive the Muslims out of Spain.

The Kingdom of Navarre

Located on the southwest slope of the Pyrenees Mountains was the medieval Kingdom of Navarre. The city of Pamplona (yes, that place where they run the bulls, but we'll get to that in a later chapter) was the capital of this small but very important kingdom in Spanish history. You see, the Kingdom of Navarre resisted both the Caliphate of Cordoba and Charlemagne's Frankish kingdom north of the Pyrenees.

Navarre serves as a testament to the freedom-loving spirit of its people, the Basques.

The Basques are descended from pre-Indo-European people who inhabited the southern slope of the Pyrenees Mountains for centuries before the Romans arrived. But once the Romans came to town and turned the entire Iberian Peninsula into Roman territory, the Basques were willing to cooperate and become part of the Roman world. They eventually converted to Christianity and became strong supporters of the Roman Catholic Church.

Yet they were still somewhat separate from their Spanish neighbors.

The Basques continued to speak their language, and although they accepted many Spanish traditions, they also kept many of their own.

As the Muslims worked their way north in Spain, conquering territory after territory, the Basques decided to fight. According to Basque legends, in 824 CE, a Basque warlord named Inigo Arista was elected King of Pamplona, the predecessor to the Kingdom of Navarre. The kings of Navarre paid tribute to the caliphs of Cordoba for a while, but by the late 10th century CE they regularly challenged Muslim authority in Spain.

The Basque royalty made marriage alliances with the other Christian kingdoms in northern Spain, which the Navarre King Sancho Garcia III (ruled 1000-1035 CE) used to lead raids into Islamic Spain.

Although Navarre would later be gobbled up by its larger neighbors, some of its early kings and knights were instrumental in turning the tide of the Reconquista in Christian Spain's favor.

This Woman Wore the Shoes in Her Family

Just a cursory glance at world history reveals that many incredible women made important advances in a variety of different fields, often against the odds. There was Margaret Thatcher in politics and government, Marie Currie in medicine and science, and Sacagawea in geography and exploration.

But perhaps no woman influenced the course of world history more than Isabella I (1451-1504 CE), the queen of Castile and later all of Spain.

Isabella was an inquisitive, intelligent girl and young woman, who used her time spent in virtual house arrest in a castle to learn about math, science, history, and logic. She eventually became the queen of Castile through a series of events that left her as the sole heir of her family's fortune and power.

But even empowered women in the late medieval/early modern period had to have a man for "cover."

At the age of 6, Isabella was betrothed to Ferdinand II of Aragon (1452-1516 CE) in what can be described as a purely political union. The Basque-descended Ferdinand was not much to look at and not particularly bright, but the union brought together the two most powerful Christian kingdoms in Spain.

There was also the little thing about the two being second cousins. You might think that cousin marriage was common in the Middle Ages—and it was, to some extent—but second cousins were considered too close by most European kingdoms as well as the Church.

The pope gave the couple a special exemption to marry and the rest is history.

Many great things took place in Spain during Isabella's rule, so let's check out a few of the most important.

1492

Isabella proved to be very active and influential on the throne, initiating policies that modernized the government and financial system. On these important points, she proved to be much more farsighted than her husband. She recognized that, for Spain to become a first-rate power, it had to be economically powerful.

For that to happen, the last of the Muslims had to be driven from the Iberian Peninsula and Spain had to look beyond the Atlantic Ocean for new trading opportunities.

Isabella and Ferdinand retook most of Spain from the Muslim forces, and by 1482 CE, the southern city of Granada was the last Islamic kingdom on the Iberian Peninsula. Known as the Emirate of Granada, its leaders decided to fight instead of fleeing to North Africa. After some pretty intense fighting, Isabella and Ferdinand's forces recaptured Granada on January 2, 1492 CE, thereby ending the Reconquista successfully for the Christians.

You probably also know that 1492 CE was an important year in Spain for another reason, due to the actions of a man named Christopher Columbus.

You might not know this, but Christopher Columbus was Italian—to be more specific, he was a citizen of the Italian city-state known as the Republic of Genoa. The explorer knew that he could make it to Asia by sailing west from Europe, but none of the kings and queens of Europe were interested in funding his expedition.

But Isabella was intrigued.

Isabella was familiar with maps drawn by Ptolemy in the 1st century CE that showed the Earth as a globe, so she knew the voyage was possible. Risking a fair amount of gold and her reputation, Isabella decided to fund Columbus' expedition.

And the rest is history.

Although Columbus didn't make it to Asia, he explored the Americas, which gave the Spanish first dibs over other countries on these mineral-rich lands. Sugar, tobacco, silver, and gold were all found there. The new lands were so valuable in resources that Spain entered into a golden era and became the most powerful country in the world.

RANDOM FACTS

1. The Vandal kings all had some pretty colorful names. The king who led the Vandals across the Pyrenees into Spain was named Gunderic. Other Vandal kings with cool names include Genseric, Huneric, and Hilderic.

2. Trajan was born in what would today be the city of Seville, Spain. He was of Roman ancestry but probably had some Spanish lineage as well.

3. Isabella became the Queen of Castile in 1474 and Queen of Aragon in 1479. She died in 1504 at the age of 53; when you consider that, it's remarkable to think what she accomplished in such a relatively short period.

4. Castilian, which is the standard form of Spanish spoken by the majority of Spanish people, is also known as "Old Spanish." The dialect of Spanish spoken in Toledo, Spain eventually became the standard for written Spanish in the 13th century CE.

5. The Nasrid Dynasty was the name of the last Islamic Dynasty in Spain. The last ruler was Muhammad XII, who surrendered to the forces of Isabella and Ferdinand in 1492.

6. The Muslims knew Spain as *Al-Andalus*. Although modern scholars are unsure of the origin of the term, there are several theories, including that it was the Arabic name for the Vandals, a derivation of the word "Atlantis," and an Arabized Visigoth/German word for Spain.

7. Isabella and Ferdinand had seven children, but only five made it to adulthood. The most famous of their children was Catherine of Aragon, who married Henry VIII of England. Queen Mary I of England was Catherine's and Henry's daughter.

8. The Visigoth kings of Spain, like the Vandals, also had some pretty interesting names. Wallia was the first king and Ardo was the last before the Muslims conquered the Iberian Peninsula in 721 CE.

9. Before the Visigoths were driven from Spain by the Muslims, the Byzantine/Eastern Roman Emperor Justinian I (ruled 527-565 CE) conquered Spain's southern Mediterranean coast in 554 CE.

10. Although the term "Hispania" was first officially used by the Romans to refer to Spain, its origins may be much older. Many scholars believe that the word is Punic/Phoenician in origin.

11. The Basques are descended from an ancient tribe known as the "Vascones," who were probably

related culturally and linguistically to the Iberians.

12. Hannibal's father, Hamilcar, brought a Carthaginian force to Spain's southern coast in 236 BCE. He was quickly able to conquer most of the Iberians on the coastline through a combination of combat, threats, and diplomacy.

13. Ferdinand was a year older than Isabella but outlived her by twelve years. Isabella's health suffered during her final few months of life and she eventually succumbed to dropsy (edema) and fever.

14. The Cave of El Castillo is another impressive Paleolithic site in Spain. Like the Altamira Cave, El Castillo has numerous cave paintings, but they are the oldest ones known.

15. The initial Islamic conquerors of Spain were from the Umayyad Caliphate, but they became an independent caliphate based in Cordoba/Cordova when the Umayyads were overthrown by the Abbasid Dynasty in 756 CE. Abd al-Rahman I (ruled 756-788 CE) was the founder of the Spanish Islamic Dynasty.

16. One of the notable features of Islamic Spain in general and Cordova, in particular, was the presence and influence of a sizable Jewish population. Most of Spain's Jews were

Sephardic, often having Spanish and Arabic names.

17. The Iberians developed scripts for their language, which have been deciphered by modern academics to a certain extent. The Iberian languages, along with Basque, are often called "Paleohispanic" languages because they predated the arrival of Indo-European languages by centuries. Today, Basque is the only surviving Paleohispanic language.

18. Although the Vandals' allies the Alans were non-Germanic, they did speak an Indo-European language that was related to Persian. The Alans settled the region of Lusitania and became known for breeding extremely large molosser hunting dogs. The Alano breed of dog is named for them.

19. In the later Middle Ages, the Kingdom of Navarre became a point of contention and, occasionally, a reason for war between France and Spain. The Bourbon Dynasty of France was established by Henry IV, who was from Navarre.

20. Today, the Spanish surname "Navarro" or "Navarra" is fairly common, but in the early modern period, few people outside of the Kingdom of Navarre would have had such a

name. People with one of those names probably have some Basque ancestry, although it may be quite distant.

Test Yourself — Questions

1. Which of these people did *not* rule early Spain?

   a. Vandals
   b. Burgundians
   c. Iberians

2. Of which kingdom was Isabella I the queen?

   a. Lusitania
   b. Seville
   c. Castile

3. The Romans referred to all of the regions in Spain collectively as?

   a. Lower Gaul
   b. Hispania
   c. Lusitania

4. Who was the Carthaginian General who conquered coastal Spain?

   a. Hamilcar
   b. Scipio
   c. Pompey

5. Which was the city the Muslim rulers of Spain used as their capital?

   a. Cordoba/Cordova
   b. Madrid
   c. Barcelona

Answers

1. b.
2. c.
3. b.
4. a.
5. a.

CHAPTER TWO:

SPAIN'S MODERN HISTORY

So, now that you know about Spain's history until about the year 1500 CE, we can move into the country's history over the last 500 years, or what is considered the "modern period." You'll no doubt find many of the facts in this chapter just as interesting in the previous one. For instance, did you know that members of the Basque ethnic group formed independence movements in the 20th century with some going as far as committing organized terrorism?

You'll read about how Spain became wealthy and powerful beyond its dream after landing in and colonizing the Americas and how that wealth came back to hurt her in the form of inflation: yes, inflation! If you do know a little about Spain's modern history already, you may have wondered, why were the Spanish neutral in both world wars? You'll find the answer in this chapter and learn that things are much more complicated—Spain wasn't exactly neutral in World War II.

Explorers and Conquistadors

Once it was realized that Christopher Columbus hadn't found a western route to Asia but instead had landed on two continents, Isabella was somewhat let down. After all, she had big plans for trade with Asia and didn't want to deal with those pesky Turks and the Silk Road.

But Isabella was smart and politically astute.

She knew that the lands in the New World could yield a remarkable amount of raw resources and that the first country to claim those lands would have an advantage. Of course, her country would probably have to fight other armies, but getting there first would surely be an advantage.

Her instincts were correct: the Portuguese were close behind.

Spain's Iberian neighbor was actually in first place in the overall exploration race in the late 15th century, having first circumnavigated Africa and establishing maritime trade routes with India. After Columbus claimed the New World for Spain, a wave of Spanish explorers and then conquerors, or *conquistadors*, traveled throughout the Americas.

Juan Ponce de Leon explored and mapped Florida after sailing on Columbus' second expedition in 1493, Alvar Nunez Cabeza de Vaca explored the Mississippi River, and Vasco Balboa was the first European to sight the Pacific Ocean from what is now Central America, proving that they had discovered continents new to Europeans.

The explorations were facilitated and sometimes funded by the activities of the bold, ruthless, and often violent conquistadors. Hernan Cortez is best known for conquering the Aztec Empire in 1521 and Francisco Pizzaro for toppling the Inca Empire in Peru in a similar fashion in 1533.

But none of the Spanish discoveries were as important as Ferdinand Magellan's trip across the globe from 1519-1521. Although Magellan was himself killed along the way, his men finished the trip, claiming more land for Spain and verifying to the skeptics that the Earth was a sphere and could be traversed.

The discoveries and conquests made Spain the most powerful country in the world but also brought many problems.

When a Good Thing Is Too Much

You might think that inflation is a purely modern concept, but it has existed since humans first began developing complex economies. Defining inflation is also quite difficult and the definition is often debated by some of the world's most eminent economists.

For the sake of our study of Spain, we'll define it as when the currency of a nation becomes devalued. The currency can become devalued in many different ways, with several potential results, but the most common outcome is an increase in the prices of commodities.

Spain was hit particularly hard by inflation beginning in the early 16th century and lasting until the mid-17th century when the problem spread to the rest of Europe. There were several root causes to this inflationary cycle, but the most apparent one was that there was simply too much silver and gold in circulation.

Spain became a victim of its own success!

Not long after the Spanish conquered most of the Americas, they found several large deposits of silver and gold there, particularly in Mexico and Peru. These mines were exploited with vigor and the metals were exported to Spain, where they were used to mint coins that served as the currency of every European nation. This all worked well for Spain for a while. It was like they had just come into an almost limitless batch of free money; but the more silver and gold that was in circulation, the less it was worth.

It simply became a case of too much of a good thing.

Spain's inflationary cycle could have been much worse, but the subsequent petering out of many of the American mines helped to raise the value of gold and silver in Europe.

But economic policies were of little worry to King Philip II of Spain, who was more concerned with conquering the world.

Spain's Most Important King

Phillip II, the King of Spain from 1556 until he died in 1598, was a physically small man but was a true giant of his age. He presided over an empire that was the largest in the modern world and it was as wealthy as it was powerful. He was king during the height of the Reformation and was violently opposed to any non-Catholics in his kingdom.

Philip was also a patron of Renaissance artists and an adherent of culture in general, but he is best remembered for his power plays.

Born to Charles I, the King of Spain and the Holy Roman Emperor, and Isabella, the Queen of Portugal, Philip was from the House of Habsburg, which would play a pivotal role in European history for several centuries. When Philip came to power, he inherited a kingdom that included the Netherlands, parts of Italy, and most of the Americas.

But Philip was always looking to add more.

He was briefly the King of England through his short marriage to Mary I (Remember her? She was his first cousin!) from 1554 to 1558 and used that status to pursue claims to territory in France.

After defeating the French in a war that lasted from 1556 to 1559, Philip cemented Spain's status as the preeminent European power when the Spanish fleet decimated the Ottoman navy in 1571 at the Battle of Lepanto. He was then crowned the King of Portugal in 1581.

Yet, as much as Philip may have expanded Spain's territory, he was also a zealous Catholic who constantly fought to protect and advance his faith.

Burn Baby Burn

There's a good chance you've heard of the Spanish Inquisition. Maybe it was in a high school or college history class where your teacher went into all the gory details of the torture the prosecutors used to get confessions and the subsequent burnings at the stake. Or maybe you remember a more humorous rendition of the Spanish Inquisition done in the 1970s British sketch comedy show, *Monty Python's Flying Circus*.

The reality is that the Spanish Inquisition was very real and it was often very brutal. More than 150,000 people were prosecuted during the Inquisition and up to 5,000 were executed.

The Spanish Inquisition began in 1478 during the reign of Ferdinand and Isabella. Although it was religious, it was for the most part controlled and carried out by the Spanish royalty, though the Catholic Church did give its blessing. Originally, the Spanish Inquisition was intended to root out heretics, but owing to Spain's religious diversity, it quickly began to be used as a weapon against the country's non-Christians.

A decree was issued in 1492 that forced the Jews of Spain to either leave the country with nothing or convert to Christianity. When Philip II came to power, he followed that up with more suppression of the *Marranos* (Sephardic Jews who had converted) and the *Moriscos* (Muslims).

The Muslims attempted one last rebellion in Granada in 1568-1570 in opposition to the Inquisition, but it was ruthlessly suppressed.

So what about all the torture associated with the Spanish Inquisition?

The stories of torture are for the most part true, although it happened less than during civil trials. Those accused of witchcraft, heresy, or being a crypto Muslim or Jew were detained and tried, which usually included some forms of torture.

Despite this, the Inquisition prohibited bloodshed in its torture sessions, only allowed sessions to last for a maximum of 15 minutes, and required a doctor to be on hand.

Since there was a prohibition on bloodshed, it meant that most people were tortured by the rack or with hot irons or coals.

Most of the accused were "allowed" to publicly admit their sins and released with fines or confiscation of some or all of their property. The most serious sentence, though, was when the punishment was "relaxation." No, this had nothing to do with vacation after the torture. It was simply when the inquisitors found the accused guilty and handed him over to the king. Many of the "relaxed" people were then burned at the stake.

If you were lucky, they strangled you to death before burning you.

That was definitely a barbeque I wouldn't want to attend!

The Modern World's First World War

The thing about nobles—no matter the period or the culture—is that they generally like to "keep it in the family" and the Spanish Habsburgs were certainly no exception to that rule. The Habsburgs believed that to keep their dynasty pure, they should marry within the family. Although there were never any brother-sister marriages in the Spanish Habsburg family, there were more than a few cousin marriages.

And that is just a bit too close for genetics.

The effects of the inbreeding were not apparent at first, but by the late 17th century the effects were becoming obvious. The kings were more and more ineffectual, culminating with the rule of Charles II (1661-1700).

Charles was known as "The Bewitched" due to his lack of mental capacity. Unfortunately for Charles, his low IQ was matched by his especially homely looks and numerous physical ailments. Since he had no heirs, the Spanish Hapsburg Dynasty ended with him, so the vultures of Europe were circling, ready to take what they could of the Spanish Empire.

The result was the Spanish War of Succession from 1701 to 1714.

Before he died, Charles handed the Spanish monarchy to Philip of France, who was of the Bourbon Dynasty. The situation didn't sit well with the British, who wanted to curb French and Spanish power in the world. The Prussians joined the British because they were eying lands in continental Europe and the Dutch saw this as a sign for them to free their entire land from Spanish rule.

Spain itself was divided among the nobility. Some wished to revive the Habsburg line, while others supported Philip, who became Philip V of Spain, and the Bourbon Dynasty.

If this all sounds confusing, it's because it is — and was! Several smaller kingdoms would temporarily support one side or the other and then drop out once things got too hot. Battles were fought not only in Europe but also in the Americas and Asia, making it the world's first true world war.

After several years of war, the Habsburgs were defeated and Philip was allowed to remain king of Spain but not France. Other notable results included the Spanish Empire in Europe being broken up, Britain becoming more powerful, and the Netherlands moved closer to the British.

Although Spain's power was severely diminished, she was able to keep her American colonies. Spain also wasn't done with Britain. When things started to get hot for the British in the Thirteen Colonies, the Spanish saw an opening to reassert their power.

Spain Supported the American Revolution

Spain's influence in Europe waned in the early years of the Spanish Bourbon Dynasty but took a drastic turn for the better under the rule of Charles III (1716-1788). Charles was a bit of a complex man — he believed in absolute rule and preserving the Spanish Empire at the expense of other nations but was also a believer in many of the Enlightenment principles of the era.

When the revolution was stirred in the American colonies, he saw a chance to forward all of those ideas.

You probably know that the French played a major role in America's fight for independence, but did you know that Spain was also involved?

After defeating Portugal in a quick war in 1777, Spain and France signed the Treaty of Aranjuez in 1779, whereby Spain agreed to support France in the American Revolution, and in return, France would help Spain recover lands from the British.

Spain was able to recover the island of Menorca in the Mediterranean and Florida in North America from the British but was unable to take Gibraltar. The Spanish also helped the Americans by shipping much-needed weapons and other materials to them from Europe. In addition, Spanish troops protected the Americans' flanks from the British by patrolling the Mississippi River and Florida.

When the Treaty of Paris was signed in 1783, ending the war, Spain came out nicely. The Spanish kept Menorca and Florida and regained some of their lost prestige.

And in America, the citizens of the young country developed a true fondness for Spain and the Spanish. Things were truly looking up for Spain at the turn of the century, but then a little guy with aspirations of world domination came along.

Dude, Where's My Empire?

Spain didn't have much time to bask in its renewed glory after the American Revolution. The French Revolution began in 1789 and lasted for ten years. It was much more brutal than the American Revolution, violently removing the French Bourbon Dynasty, which eventually resulted in Napoleon Bonaparte becoming France's military dictator.

The Spanish may have been opposed to the British, but they were equally opposed to revolutionary sentiments.

Spain initially fought against Napoleon's France in the War of the First Coalition (1792-1797) but lost decisively in 1795 and decided to reassess its allies and options. The Spanish agreed to give Napoleon Louisiana and its land west of the Mississippi River in addition to what would become the Dominican Republic.

This was just the beginning of the precipitous decline of the Spanish Empire.

After Spain proved to be a less than able ally,

Napoleon invaded Spain and occupied it until 1814. The Spanish rebelled, fought an intense guerilla campaign against the French, and eventually drove the invaders out and restored Bourbon rule, but the damage was too much for the Spanish Empire to survive.

Spain's colonies saw the American Revolution as inspiration and the events of the Napoleonic Wars as a sign to assert their own independence. By 1826, the only major colonial possessions that Spain still held were Cuba, Puerto Rico, and the Philippines.

Just like that, Spain's mighty empire had disappeared and there was no getting it back!

Florida Has Some Nice Beaches

When the dust settled after the Napoleonic Wars, there was a new order in Europe: Great Britain was the most powerful country, Russia's power and stature had risen, and although France was technically the loser, it retained much of its influence on the continent.

Spain was the real loser.

Spain's infrastructure was ravaged, a large share of its male population had perished, and its GDP had been reduced to record lows. The combination of years of warfare on Spanish soil and the loss of its American empire had made Spain one of the poorest and least developed of all European nations, with no relief in sight.

Even eternally backward and eastward-looking Russia was doing better!

Spain's post-Napoleonic Wars poverty led to extreme social problems that erupted in the form of violent rebellions. The monarchy knew that it had to do something drastic to put some money into its coffers. The king's financial advisors suggested selling some of Spain's few remaining colonial possessions to either the British or Americans.

Neither country had much interest in the Philippines at the time and the Spanish wanted to keep Cuba and Puerto Rico because they were lucrative and home to many Spanish subjects.

So, the Spanish thought, "Let's sell the Yanks that worthless piece of swampland known as Florida."

In 1821, under the terms of the Adams-Onís Treaty that was signed in 1819, the United States bought Florida from Spain for a cool $5 million. That may sound like a steal for the Americans, and it was when you consider the long-term, but the Spanish truly thought they were just getting rid of some worthless swampland. They had little infrastructure developed in Florida and there were just as many American settlers there as Spanish ones.

Florida was also full of hostile Seminoles who didn't

care for the Spanish or Americans.

The Spanish had no idea that in just over 100 years, Florida would become a vacation hotspot and retirement destination for millions of Americans.

Well, maybe if they knew that, they would've sold it anyway.

Carlos' Way

Spain's problems in the 1820s didn't get any better after it sold Florida to the Americans. Soldiers rebelled in Cadiz and the French invaded Spain in 1823 once more and occupied parts of it until 1828. Then, in 1833, Ferdinand VII died, leaving the country ripe for civil war.

Once more, Spain was a hot mess!

On the one side were supporters of Ferdinand VII's wife, Maria Cristina, who was ruling on behalf of her infant daughter. On the other was an equally powerful faction supporting Prince Carlos/Charles V as the rightful heir to the throne. He was Ferdinand's younger brother, a staunch Catholic, and conservative who wished to bring back Spain's former glories.

Fighting between the two factions began in 1833 and ended in 1840 after Prince Carlos fled Spain to exile.

Although Prince Carlos never attempted to win back the throne, he had many supporters throughout Spain, especially in the northern regions. His supporters were also willing to stir things up and cause problems in the hopes that they would get another one of his family members, a "Carlist," on the Spanish throne.

There was a Second Carlist War from 1846-1849 and a Third Carlist War from 1872-1876, but the Liberals were able to win both wars and hold onto power.

Just when it seemed as though the Carlists and conservatives would never be able to regain power, the winds of change began to sweep across Europe. Socialism and fascism became popular movements in many countries, including Spain, which the Carlists planned to use to their advantage.

But exactly how would the Carlists fit into this new political paradigm in Europe?

Two Countries Going in Opposite Directions

The year 1898 proved to be monumental for both Spain and the United States but due to different reasons. It was in that year that the United States finally became a true world power by acquiring territories off the mainland, while Spain lost what little it had left of its empire.

This might be familiar from your high school or college history classes; I'm talking about the Spanish-American War. The war itself was not "major" in terms of its length or casualties—only about 800 Spaniards and 385 Americans were killed in fighting over three months—but its long-term repercussions were major for both countries.

The war helped establish American identity as a tough country that others wouldn't mess with, which was exemplified by the actions of future president Theodore Roosevelt, who led his troops up San Juan Hill yelling, "Remember the Maine!" The Americans came to the aid of the rebelling Cubans and thoroughly defeated a Spanish army that had little will to fight.

The Americans also defeated the Spanish in the Philippines.

As a result of the war, the Americans gained the Philippines, Puerto Rico, and Cuba—temporarily, before granting Cuba independence in 1902.

The war left nearly everyone in Spain—on all ends of the political spectrum—with a sour taste in their mouths. Those on the left viewed the loss of empire as a sign to focus on social programs at home. Some even wanted to abolish the monarchy or at the very least reduce the Church's influence in the government. The right saw the losses as a betrayal and proof that Spain had grown weak over the last 100 years.

Interestingly, most agreed that the spirit, fortitude, and bravery the Americans showed in the war was something that was lacking in Spain, although it was not absent.

The disparate political parties disagreed on how to get that spirit back though, and as time went by, they began to view each other increasingly as the enemy.

Spain Was Neutral in Both World Wars

Spain's political and social problems continued into the 20th century and were in many ways aggravated by the new political movements spreading across Europe. Many of the Liberals began to gravitate toward socialist, communist, and anarchist ideologies, while some Carlists saw fascism as an answer to Spain's problems.

The country was drifting toward more conflict, but by 1913, most Spaniards were more interested in rebuilding their country and moving on from the disasters of the 19th century than they were in being involved in another wide-ranging conflict. As the winds of World War I, or the "Great War," as it was known at the time, began swirling over Europe and alliances were being made, there was some pressure put on Spain to pick a side.

But Spanish Prime Minister Eduardo Dato publicly declared his nation's neutrality after the war began.

This doesn't mean that the Spanish didn't have their

opinions on the war.

In a pattern that would largely play out in the upcoming Spanish Civil War, those on the left-wing of the political spectrum generally supported France, while the right-wing was in favor of Germany. There were some Spaniards who volunteered to fight in the French Foreign Legion, but most of the Spanish population decided to sit the war out and concentrate on rebuilding their nation.

Spanish industry surged during World War I, as the government and private Spanish companies sold supplies to both sides. The economy did fairly well; so well, in fact, that inflation became a problem again, putting the break on some of the country's economic advance. Still, overall, the choice to remain neutral was probably a good one.

Spain also decided to stay neutral in World War II. Well, sort of. That story is a little trickier and can only be understood in the context of the Spanish Civil War.

So, let's take a look at that.

The Spanish Civil War

Without a doubt, the most defining event of Spain's modern history was the Spanish Civil War. Lasting from 1936 to 1939, the war pitted political factions from the left against the right, dividing regions, cities, villages, and even families.

The war began after a fairly complex series of events. King Alfonso XIII allowed free elections in 1931 to replace the existing dictatorship, which resulted in left-wing parties winning control of the government and declaring a republic. Political violence continued between the right and left, with the result being a shift in the electorate to the right-wing parties in 1933.

Things only got worse from there.

The left took power again in 1936, but an attempted right-wing military coup pushed things over the top—Spain quickly found itself in a full-scale civil war!

On one side was a coalition of socialists, communists, anarchists, and various other liberals who supported the government. They became known as "the Republicans." Opposing the Republicans was an alliance of monarchists, conservatives, and—most notably—a fascist organization known as "the Falange." The right-wing alliance was called "the Nationalists."

The fighting was particularly brutal: over 100,000 Nationalists died in action, more than 175,000 Republicans were killed fighting, and nearly 200,000 civilians were killed. Cities were devastated, villages were wiped off the map, and more than 20,000 churches were destroyed by the Republicans.

The Republicans had numerical superiority and controlled the east coast and the Basque country, but the Nationalists were better prepared as their leadership came from the military establishment.

The Spanish Civil War also proved to be a "proxy war" for the larger geopolitical situation unfolding in Europe. The Soviet Union sent gold, advisors, and pilots to the Republicans, while Nazi Germany and Fascist Italy sent more than 60,000 men to support the Nationalists.

About 60,000 international volunteers came to Spain to fight on the Republican side. Most of the Republican volunteers were idealistic leftists who saw Republican Spain as a stepping-stone to a future socialist utopia and the Nationalists as another potential fascist nation in the growing Axis powers. Traveling among the volunteers was American writer Ernest Hemmingway, who wrote the screenplay for the 1937 film, *The Spanish Earth*. Although Hemmingway never fired a gun for the Republicans, *The Spanish Earth* is considered to be a pro-Republican propaganda film.

Other well-known writers, such as George Orwell, took up the Republican cause in combat, but they were often disillusioned by the atrocities committed by both sides.

By early 1939, the Nationalist forces, led by General Francisco Franco, captured the province of Catalonia, which marked the beginning of the end for the Republicans. Franco declared victory in April, sending a wave of Republican refugees out of Spain.

Spain had a new strong man and things were about to change.

Dictators Usually Have Mustaches

If you take a look at some of the more notorious dictators from the 20th century, you'll notice a common theme. Vladimir Lenin had a mustache-goatee thing going on that kind of made him look like Lucifer, while his successor Josef Stalin also had a conspicuously bushy 'stache.

Of course, Hitler was known for that little mustache that was all the rage throughout Europe for a time, until he ruined it.

Mussolini, though, was bald, so I guess he is the exception to our rule.

Meanwhile, Francisco Franco, the dictator of Spain from 1939 until he died in 1975, usually wore a "pencil-thin" style mustache. Franco's mustache may be somewhat of a laughing matter, but his rule certainly wasn't for many Spaniards.

Franco was born into an upper-class military family in 1892 in the northwest province of Galicia. He went into the family business by embarking on a career in the military, eventually becoming the youngest general in modern European history at age 33. Although he was not raised in a particularly religious family, Franco was an ardent Catholic (at least outwardly) and eventually came to support fascist and nationalist groups that opposed the Republican government.

He wholeheartedly supported the attempted coup against the Republican government and became the Nationalists' leading general in the Spanish Civil War.

After the war, Franco assumed the role of dictator, or *caudillo*, until his death but was hesitant to fully accept the fascist mantle. He developed good relations with Fascist Italy and Nazi Germany but never fully joined their club and maintained relations with the rest of the West.

Spain was one of the only nations in the world to be officially neutral during World War II. Franco maintained diplomatic and commercial ties with Germany, Italy, and Japan. Many historians describe his overall stance during World War II as attempting to play both sides. Franco allowed volunteers to fight alongside the Axis powers on the Eastern Front but not on the Western Front. He allowed thousands of Jews to safely pass through Spain but then limited their number of visas when pressured by Germany.

The reality is that Franco's Machiavellian policies paid off.

Once the war was over, Spain—and Argentina to a certain extent—stood as the only quasi-fascist states in the world. The West allowed Franco to continue his policies of political repression against his opponents because most were sick of war. He was also viewed as a potential ally against communism in the Cold War.

So, Franco rounded up his enemies and gave former Nazis asylum. He gradually liberalized Spain's economy and, by the time he died, the country seemed to be headed toward joining the rest of the nations in Western Europe in the new political order.

But the Basques of northern Spain had a few things to say about that.

Euskadi Ta Askatasuna

Remember the Basques and the role they played in Spain's early history? Well, when Spain had its tough years in the 1800s, the Basques suffered through it along with the rest of the people. Then, when the Spanish Civil War happened, most Basques took the side of the Republicans. It was kind of a strange position in which the Basques found themselves. Traditionally a very religious and pro-Catholic people, the Basques sided with the antireligious Republicans because their government gave the community of Basque Country what they wanted: more autonomy.

Conversely, most on the right wanted to more fully integrate Basque Country into Spain and some of the fascists—such as the Falange—saw the Basques as outsiders and as a threat to order.

When the Spanish Civil War ended, it only seemed to confuse the Basques' position in Spain. Franco took an especially tough stance on the Basques and Basque Country by repressing any hint of an independence movement. However, as so often happens when authorities use repression, this tactic inadvertently created organized, armed resistance.

In 1959, Euskadi Ta Askatasuna formed.

Euskadi Ta Askatasuna is the Basque language name of "Basque Country and Freedom," often abbreviated simply as "ETA." ETA was a purely political organization for several years, refining its increasingly left-wing and Marxist ideology. By the time ETA committed its first violent act in 1968, it was similar in structure, tactics, and ideology to other leftist terrorist groups in Europe at the time, such as the IRA, the Red Brigades, and the Red Army Faction.

ETA's campaign of violence included targeted assassinations and bombings, which took the lives of

829 people, mainly in Spain but also in France and Portugal. Due to its violent actions, ETA was declared a terrorist group by many western countries, including the United States and the United Kingdom. Although the Basque independence movement had support around the world, ETA's violence probably hurt the movement more than anything.

ETA finally called a ceasefire in 2010 and formally disbanded in 2018. Although many former ETA members have been released from prison, some are still incarcerated for a host of violent crimes.

The idea of an independent Basque state is still the dream of many, but it looks like it will be a while before that dream is ever realized.

Spain and the European Union

If there's one thing you should have learned by now about Spain's history—besides that it's very exciting—is that things there changed very quickly. If you were a Spaniard living in most periods of history and didn't like the way things were, it usually wouldn't be a problem; things wouldn't stay the same for very long.

This was true for the upper classes as well as the people struggling to survive.

After Franco died, open elections were held and Spain slowly began integrating itself into European affairs. It joined NATO and the European Community and finally the European Union (EU).

On January 1, 1999, the peseta was replaced as Spain's currency with the euro, thereby cementing the nation's role as a member in the EU.

Spain's economy took off in the 1980s, but it was hit hard by the worldwide recession in the late 2000s. As a member of the EU, the Spanish government was somewhat constrained as to how it dealt with the repercussions of the recession, especially its chronically high unemployment. You see, since Spain is a member of the EU, it is reliant on the organization for its currency and it must follow certain guidelines in terms of deficit spending.

The Germans, French, Dutch, and other more powerful members of the EU generally require Spain and the other less powerful members to follow austerity measures, which may keep the budgets balanced and put a lid on inflation, but they can also hurt employment rates.

Despite these problems, Spain would be one of the last nations to leave the EU.

RANDOM FACTS

1. Although most of the Spanish-American War was fought in the Caribbean, there were actions in the Pacific as well. The biggest battle in the Pacific was the Battle of Manila Bay on May 1, 1898, in the Philippines. The more modern American Navy decisively defeated the antiquated Spanish Navy. It was the last major battle in the Spanish-American War and the end of Spanish influence in the Philippines.

2. Ferdinand Magellan was Portuguese but made his circumnavigation of the globe under the Spanish flag. In a situation similar to that of Columbus, the king of Portugal thought that Magellan's expedition was doomed to fail so he refused to fund it. After Magellan was killed by natives in the Philippines, the circumnavigation was completed by Spaniard Juan Sebastian Elcano.

3. American volunteers in the Spanish Civil War formed the Abraham Lincoln Battalion. The Lincoln Battalion was the 17th battalion of the XV International Brigade that fought for the Republicans.

4. The Adams-Onís Treaty was named for its two

major negotiators: Secretary of State and future American President John Q. Adams and Spanish diplomat Luis de Onís y González-Vara.

5. After Franco died, the government of Spain created a new constitution in 1978, which is still in effect.

6. Like Columbus, explorer Amerigo Vespucci was an Italian by birth, but he sailed first for Portugal and later for Spain. Vespucci is credited as being the first person to figure out that the Americas were not part of Asia. Vespucci became a Spanish citizen and died in Seville, Spain in 1512.

7. In 1588, the Spanish attempted to invade England with their mighty naval armada. It didn't end so well for the Spanish! No country even came close to an attempted invasion of England until World War II.

8. On December 10, 1898, the Americans and Spanish signed the Treaty of Paris, which officially ended the Spanish-American War. The Americans gave the Spanish $20 million for the Philippines.

9. The Spanish were assisted by the Venetian Navy at the Battle of Lepanto. Spain, Venice, the Vatican, and several smaller Catholic kingdoms comprised an alliance known as "the Holy

League." The purpose of the Holy League was to break Ottoman power in the Mediterranean, and although it was decisively successful at the Battle of Lepanto, it failed to achieve its long-term goals.

10. The Royal Alcazar of Madrid has served as a royal seat of power in Spain for quite some time, but it grew in importance and stature after the Reconquista in the 16th century. The palace was originally built as a fortress by the Muslims in the 9th century.

11. Although the Spanish Inquisition took place during the Reformation and can only be understood in that context, there were very few Protestants to prosecute. The Spanish Inquisition also prosecuted far fewer people for witchcraft than in other European countries. The primary targets of the Spanish Inquisition were former Jews, or *conversos*, who were thought to be practicing their former religion in private.

12. Contrary to common belief, silver was used for most Spanish coins. There were several different currency reforms in Spain from the 16th century to the present, with the result being the use of different types of coins, including the real and the escudo. Today Spain uses the euro.

13. Hernando de Soto (1500-1542) is one of the most

accomplished but lesser known of all the Spanish explorers and conquistadors. He led major expeditions in central and South America before exploring what would become Florida and the southeastern United States. Many towns, counties, and rivers are named after him, including De Soto County, Mississippi and Hernando, Mississippi.

14. Spain has had traditionally high unemployment rates in the decades since Franco's death. It was below 10% just before the global financial crisis in 2009 but jumped back up above 20%, which is where it remains in early 2020.

15. ETA's deadliest attack was the June 19, 1987 bombing of the Hipercor shopping center in Barcelona, Spain. The attack killed 21 people and injured 45.

16. Franco died of heart failure on November 20, 1975 at the age of 82. He was interred at the Valle de los Caídos military cemetery, but the government decided to move his remains in November 2019.

17. It is often forgotten that the tiny Pacific island of Guam was once part of the Spanish Empire. The Spanish lost it to the Americans in the Spanish-American War.

18. The successful American-French siege of

Yorktown during the American Revolution was financially facilitated by the Spanish. Spanish military officer Francisco Saavedra de Sangronis raised more than 500,000 silver pesos in Havana that were used to buy supplies for the war effort.

19. The Spanish government attempted to settle Florida twice. The first attempt ended when the British bought Florida in 1763, but Spain regained it in 1783 due to being on the winning side of the American Revolution. Due to problems with its economy and independence movements around the Americas, Spain decided to get something from Florida rather than losing it to the Americans for nothing.

20. The region of Catalonia—and its largest city, Barcelona—was a hotbed of Republican activity during the Spanish Civil War. Barcelona fell to the Nationalists after a siege on January 26, 1939.

Test Yourself — Questions

1. What is the acronym for the now-defunct Basque terrorist group?

    a. ETA
    b. IRA
    c. PTA

2. Who was the dictator of Spain from 1939 until he died in 1975?

    a. Benito Mussolini
    b. Francisco Franco
    c. Antonio Banderas

3. What was the name of the war that passed power in Spain from the Habsburg to the Bourbon Dynasty?

    a. Spanish Civil War
    b. American Revolution
    c. Spanish War of Succession

4. Spain began using which currency in 1999?

    a. Pound
    b. Peso
    c. Euro

5. The Spanish defeated the Ottoman Turks in which major sea battle in 1571?

    a. Battle of the Sea
    b. Battle of Lepanto
    c. Battle of Gibraltar

Answers

1. a.
2. b.
3. c.
4. c.
5. b.

CHAPTER THREE:

SPAIN'S GEOGRAPHY, CLIMATE, AND INDUSTRY

After reading the first two chapters about Spain's history, you're now a lot more familiar with its geography than you may think. For instance, you should know that Madrid has been Spain's capital for most of its history and that Cadiz and Barcelona are also important coastal cities. You also know that, along with Portugal, Spain is a peninsula, which means that it is a landmass surrounded on three sides by water. In this chapter, we'll take a more in-depth look into some of those and other interesting geographical facts about Spain. It is important to know that geography concerns, not just landmasses and population distribution, but also climate, weather, politics, and culture. And, after reading this chapter, you'll see that although Spain is somewhat average in size for a modern country, at nearly 195,000 square miles, it is quite diverse in its topography, climate, and culture.

The Pyrenees Mountains separate Spain from France

The Pyrenees Mountains stretch 305 miles across Spain's northern border from the Bay of Biscay in the west to the Catalonian coast on the Mediterranean Sea on the east. The Pyrenees are a true alpine range, with summits of more than 11,000 feet and snowcapped peaks year-round.

The Pyrenees served as a natural barrier between Spain and the rest of Europe, which both hurt and helped Spain in some ways. It helped the Spanish because it limited invasions from Europe, but when Islamic invaders came from the south, it essentially locked the outsiders in.

There is little doubt that the Pyrenees are full of important history. The name is derived from a Greek mythological princess, and ever since ancient times, it has served as a key historical site, where warriors such as Hannibal rode elephants and Crusader monarchs like Isabella and Ferdinand began their quest to win back Spain for the Church.

The Pyrenees were once home to an incredible amount of wildlife and are still home to a fair amount of flora and fauna. Perhaps one of the most incredible natural features of the Pyrenees Mountains is the large number of waterfalls found throughout the chain.

An interesting aspect of the Pyrenees that has caused consternation to engineers over the centuries is its lack of natural mountain passes. Because of this, most of the major roads that connect Spain to the rest of Europe are near either coastline. So, if you're thinking about road tripping through the heart of the Pyrenees, be prepared to take some extra time because the roads are snaky and it can take a while to get from point A to point B.

But if Hannibal could do it with a bunch of stubborn elephants, I'm sure you can do it in a car, right?

The Pillars of Hercules

If you ever take a Mediterranean Cruise and pass through the Strait of Gibraltar, you'll see why the Greeks called it "The Pillars of Hercules." On the European side, you'll see the Rock of Gibraltar jutting out into the sea, and on the African side, you'll notice Jebel Musa. When these two landmarks are viewed as a panorama, they resemble two large pillars.

The Strait of Gibraltar is where the southernmost tip of Spain and Gibraltar are separated from Africa by a 36-mile-long strait of the Mediterranean Sea that is less than nine miles wide at its narrowest point.

You may be surprised to learn that, although Gibraltar is connected to Spain and has been part of

Spain for most of its history, it has been a British colony since 1704, when the British took it during the Spanish War of Succession.

Perhaps fittingly, just across the strait, surrounded by Morocco, is the Spanish colonial city of Ceuta. The Spanish took control of Ceuta in 1668 after the Portuguese relinquished control.

Daily ferry services connect cities on the Spanish side to the Moroccan coast and there have even been talks between the two governments of building an undersea transportation tunnel similar to the one underneath the English Channel. Reaction to the proposed tunnel has been lukewarm at best, though.

Why would you want to travel underground when you can see the beautiful Pillars of Hercules during your commute?

Did You Know Spain Is a Constitutional Monarchy Unitary State?

That may sound like a lot, but it's pretty simple. It just means that, although Spain still has a king or queen, the true power is in its bicameral (two-tiered) system of government. The Congress of Deputies is the lower house of the Congress, whose members are elected by popular vote and serve four-year terms. The Senate is the upper house and, as in most other countries with a similar government composition, it has fewer members. Most of the 259 Senators are chosen by direct vote, although 51 are selected by their regional legislatures.

The Prime Minister is the head of government but also like in Britain, the king or queen is the head of state.

So, that explains Spain's government, but how does the government wield that power?

Well, Spain is classified as a "unitary state," which means that its central government is powerful and decides things for the provinces and smaller government units. This is different from a federal state—the United States, Canada, Australia, Argentina, and Germany for example—where the provinces or states within a country have certain powers and/or rights that are delineated in the national constitution.

As with everything, of course, there are plenty of gray areas.

Spain is comprised of seventeen "autonomous communities" that are further divided into 50 provinces. This status allows the various ethnicities, such as the Basques, and regions such as Catalonia, to have a certain amount of independence.

Now you might be thinking, "Doesn't that make it a federal state then?"

You would think so, but it doesn't. Technically speaking, Spain's government is a "decentralized unitary state" like that of France or Britain. The different provinces may have more freedom, but the central government still makes all of the laws.

Llívia is Spain's Version of Alaska

Well, sort of. Llívia may not be much like Alaska in terms of size or climate, but both places share the unique geographical trait of being *exclaves*. An exclave is simply a state or province—or town, in Llívia's case—that is surrounded by the borders of another nation-state.

The small town of Llívia, Spain is part of the province of Catalonia but is separated by the rest of Spain by about one mile, as it is surrounded by France. The sleepy Spanish-speaking population of the town is about 1,500 today. Remarkably, this population has remained fairly stable throughout most of modern history. Llívia has had an uncanny ability to stay out of most of the major wars that have gripped Spain and France.

It avoided being ruled by the Moors for most of the Middle Ages and was instead part of different French principalities, although, under the Treaty of the Pyrenees of 1659, it was ceded to the Kingdom of Spain. The town avoided most of the major atrocities during the Spanish Civil War and quickly integrated into the European Union in the 1990s.

Llívia is a truly charming locale, situated on the northern slope of the Pyrenees Mountains. The climate is moderate and the people are friendly and generally open to strangers.

The openness of Llívia's people is no doubt partly due to the town's unique geographic situation.

Cars, Tourism, and Wine Are Big Business in Spain

Tourism and the automotive industry combine to make up about 20% of Spain's GDP, with the tourism industry taking a slightly larger share. With all of Spain's history, great beaches on the Atlantic and Mediterranean coasts, mountains, forests, and some incredible nightlife in the larger cities, it is no wonder that so many foreigners come there for vacations. For several decades now, Spain has been a major destination for British tourists and retirees who find that their money buys much more in Spain than it does in other places in Europe.

Spain as a major tourist destination is well known, but did you know that Spain is also a major automobile manufacturer?

Lower costs of living, labor, and taxes have all made Spain a desirable location for many automotive companies from around the world to open factories.

Along with the pharmaceuticals, vehicles are the country's primary export. Close to three million vehicles are produced every year in Spain, with about 80% of those destined for export. Spain has two native automotive manufacturers, PSA and SEAT, but it is also home to American, German, and French automobile manufacturing companies.

Spain is also known for producing Mediterranean crops in its coastal areas, including oranges, olives, and mandarins. Of course, since Spain has a climate and topography similar to some areas of Italy and France, it is also known for its wine. Many Spaniards will argue that although wine may not bring as much money as cars into their country, it is the most important export.

Spanish wine may come in behind French and Italian wines in total exports, but most Spaniards will argue—and some will even fist-fight—if you refute that their wine is the best!

Bears, Wolves, and Ibexes

You might not think of Spain as being home to a large amount of wildlife but, compared to the rest of western Europe, it has sizable breeding populations of different species, especially in the Pyrenees and the Cantabrian Mountains of northwestern Spain. Unfortunately, many species have been hunted to or near extinction, either because they were viewed as dangerous or as a pest—as with wolves and bears— or to consume their meat, as with ibexes.

Many people are surprised to learn that brown bears, known as "grizzlies" in the U.S. and Canada, are native to Spain. The largest population of brown bears in Spain is in the Cantabrian Range, which is a 190-mile range just west of the Pyrenees. It is believed that between 200 and 300 brown bears live in this region. Brown bears also live in the Pyrenees, but there is believed to be less than 50 despite efforts to increase the population.

Europeans have long had a love-hate relationship with wolves, hunting them to extinction in some parts but also often incorporating them into coats of arms and national symbols. Spain is no different in this respect. Spain is home to up to 3,000 members of the grey wolf subspecies known as the Iberian or Spanish wolf. Most of the wolves inhabit the northwestern portion of Spain and Portugal, which includes lowlands as well as mountainous areas north of the Douro River.

Spain is also home to several species of prey animals, most notably the ibex. The Iberian ibex is a type of wild goat that lives primarily in the southern and eastern highlands of Spain. Known for its long curving horns and ability to rocky, inaccessible locations, the Iberian ibex was heavily hunted for its meat. It once had four subspecies, but the

Portuguese and Pyrenean subspecies have gone extinct.

There has been an attempt to revive the Pyrenean subspecies through cloning, but that's something we'll talk about a little later.

From Freezing to Sunburn by Lunchtime

Yes, it is true! You can begin your morning in the highest peaks of the Pyrenees or the Sierra Nevada range in the southern province of Granada, which both have cold alpine climates, work your way down the mountains to the coast of Catalonia or Granada and find yourself in a hot-summer Mediterranean climate with temperatures in the 80s F. These temperature extremes make Spain one of the ten most climatically diverse countries in the world, as it has 13 distinct Köppen climate zones.

The majority of Spain falls in the hot-summer Mediterranean climate zone, which as the name indicates, is marked by hot summers and mild winters.

The second-largest climate zone in Spain is known as the oceanic zone. Although the name seems to denote a climate affected by the ocean, most of the area in Spain in this zone is in the northern provinces and not near either the Atlantic or Mediterranean. This is the same climate zone that covers most of France and England, so it is marked by cooler temperatures and more precipitation.

Large areas of central and southern Spain fall under the semiarid climate zone. These areas are prone to higher temperatures and less rainfall, which leaves less vegetation. Within this zone is the Tabernas Desert in Almira province of southern Spain. Although only covering about 110 square miles, the Tabernas Desert has several sub-climate zones, including hot desert, hot semi-arid and cold desert, and cold semi-arid desert in the lowland areas. In many ways, the Tabernas Desert is a microcosm of Spain's diverse climate zones.

Madrid Is Spain's Capital and Largest City

Located almost directly in the middle of Spain on the Manzares River is Madrid, the capital and largest city in Spain. The city itself has nearly 3,225,000 inhabitants and its metro area comprises more than six million people, which makes it the third-largest city in the EU.

Madrid's size, location, and cultural background all combine to make it one of the most vibrant and important cities not just in Europe, but in the entire world. Investors from all corners of the globe have been drawn to Madrid due to lower costs and the city has also served as a sort of cultural beacon for the Spanish-speaking world. Spanish language movies and television shows produced in Madrid are routinely screened throughout Latin America and, in turn, Latin American tourists and immigrants often make Madrid their first stop when they visit Europe.

Madrid's history can be traced back to the contentious period of the Reconquista during the Middle Ages. The city was first built as a fortress by the Muslims, but after the Christians retook the region, they developed it into a city. The origin of the name "Madrid" is unknown, but many believe that it is Arabic, having to do with the Manzares River.

Due to its central location in Spain, Madrid quickly grew into a major city and in 1561 it became the capital of the Kingdom of Spain. Madrid has been the capital of Spain ever since and is home to both houses of Spain's national government. It is also where the Spanish royal family lives.

Due to its status as a national capital, as well as being an important financial and cultural center, rents can be kind of high in Madrid, but the standard of living is also high and crime is fairly low.

And, of course, Madrid has plenty of nightlife options, but we'll talk about some of those in another chapter.

Two Island Chains Belong to Spain

In addition to the Spanish mainland, two

archipelagos are considered part of Spain. One is the Balearic Islands in the Mediterranean Sea and the other is the Canary Islands in the Atlantic Ocean.

The Balearic Islands are comprised of dozens of islands that cover nearly 2,000 square miles, ranging from 50 to 190 miles off the Catalan coast of northeast Spain. Due to the proximity to Catalonia, the islands are heavily influenced by Catalonian culture, with Catalan being spoken there as frequently as Spanish.

Although the archipelago contains dozens of islands, Mallorca, Menorca (remember that one?), Ibiza, and Formentera are the largest and home to the majority of the islands' more than one million citizens.

The Balearic Islands are known for their sunny Mediterranean weather, beautiful landscapes, and affordable prices. The islands are associated with their long history of hosting different occupiers. As with mainland Spain, the Balearic Islands were ruled by Phoenicians, Carthaginians, Romans, Vandals, Visigoths, and the Moors all before the modern period.

Located about 60 miles off the southwest coast of Morocco—but still an autonomous community of Spain, and therefore, still politically part of Europe—is the archipelago known as the Canary Islands.

The "Canaries," as they are commonly called, are

slightly larger than the Balearics with seven major islands, numerous smaller ones, and an area of nearly 3,000 square miles. The Canaries also have about double the population of the Balearics. More than 900,000 people live on the largest island, Tenerife, and more than 800,000 live on the second largest island, Gran Canaria.

The Canaries were first settled in ancient times by a Berber people known as the Guanche and they remained somewhat isolated due to the islands' distance from the more advanced cultures of the ancient Mediterranean. The Spanish took control of the islands in the 1400s and used them as a waypoint for their early exploration and colonization of the Americas.

Today, the Canaries are famed for their mild weather, banana crops, and the fact that they have two capitals—Santa Cruz de Tenerife on Tenerife and Las Palmas de Gran Canaria on Gran Canaria.

What's Up with Catalonia?

You may remember back in 2017 there were protests in the autonomous community of Catalonia in northeast Spain. If you do remember those protests, then you'll probably remember that many of the protesters were attractive, healthy-looking people who seemed particularly well-dressed for pro-independence protests that occasionally turned into riots. Yes, it literally seemed to be like a day at the beach for many of the Catalan protesters, so when the Spanish authorities got serious, most of the protesters went home and we haven't heard much from Catalonia since.

But what was behind those protests?

Well, Catalonia is one of Spain's 17 autonomous communities and within it there are four provinces: Barcelona, Girona, Lleida, and Tarragona. Barcelona is also Spain's second-largest city.

The Catalonian independence issue that arose in 2017 is primarily because Catalonia has always been a little different from the rest of Spain, and its people are very cognizant of that fact.

The Catalan language developed from Latin during the Middle Ages, as Spanish did, but it retained its unique status even when Catalonia became part of Spain. Today, most Catalans speak both Spanish and Catalan, but they prefer to speak their native language.

Traditionally, the unemployment rates are lower in Catalonia and the economy is generally stronger than in the rest of Spain.

Culture, though, is where Catalonia tends to separate itself most prominently from the rest of Spain. Besides the language difference, Catalans tend to be more northern European in some of their manners and cultural habits. For instance, the easy-going nature found in most of Spain—where, for instance, it is common to come late to a dinner party—is far less common in Catalonia. Catalans also tend to be more politically liberal and far less religious than other Spaniards.

Still, despite the cultural differences, it's obvious that most Catalans aren't willing to die to separate their provinces from Spain. For the time being, it appears that Catalonia will continue to be part of the Kingdom of Spain.

The Meseta Central Is Surrounded by Mountains

The Meseta Central, or Inner Plateau, is located in central Spain and covers more than 210,000 square miles. The plateau's elevations average more than a mile and it is enclosed by mountains ranges: the Cantabrian Mountains to its north, the Sistema Penibetico to its south, the Sistema Iberico to its east, and the Sistema Central to its west.

The basins of the Duero, Tagus, and Guadiana rivers are also located in the Meseta Central.

Since the Sistema Central cuts into the middle of the plateau, it divides it into a northern and southern basin.

Although the Inner Plateau is the single largest area of Spain, it is the least agriculturally diverse due to its lack of rainfall and rocky soil. Still, large farms have produced wheat in the region going back to the Roman Era, and thanks to modern irrigation techniques, the variety of crops grown there have increased in recent decades. Several successful orchards operate in the plateau and large livestock operations are also common.

If you travel through Spain by car or rail, then chances are you'll go through the Meseta Central. If so, enjoy the quaint landscapes and panoramas of mountain chains in the background.

Spain Shares a Border with Five Countries, Sort of

Spain shares nearly 1,200 miles of borders with France, Portugal, Andorra, and Morocco. Of those, Gibraltar isn't a real country but is instead a colony of Britain and has been part of Spain for most of its history.

And it only shares three-quarters of a mile border with Spain.

Since Spain does not recognize Britain's claim to Gibraltar, there is a fence along the border, unlike the rest of Spain's borders. Although Britain and Spain are both in the EU, the competing claims and the fact that Britain is set to leave the EU means that the tiny border will probably be even more policed in the future.

Spain shares a sea border with Morocco but also a short land border of just under 12 miles. Remember Ceuta? Well, that city—along with the Spanish town of Melilla—form the land border between Spain and Morocco.

Have you ever heard of Andorra? Don't feel bad if you haven't! It's a tiny "microstate" located along Spain's northeast border with France. Andorra is so tiny that its border with Spain is only about 40 miles. If you're roading tripping through the northern slope of the Pyrenees in Catalonia, don't blink, because you might miss Andorra!

Spain's largest and most powerful neighbor is France. Apart from the 40 miles of Andorra, France comprises all of Spain's northern border at just over 400 miles. The culture of the French side of the Spanish-French border is very similar to Spain's, with a large number of Basques calling the region their home.

Spain shares its longest border with Portugal at just over 750 miles. Spain and Portugal combine to comprise the Iberian Peninsula, and despite some historical rivalries and linguistic differences, they share quite a bit culturally, although not all Spaniards or Portuguese would agree with that, especially when it comes to Olivenza.

Olivenza is a small municipality on the southwest Spanish-Portuguese border. Currently, Spain controls Olivenza, but Portugal claims it as well.

Despite the competing claims, don't worry — there is very little chance that the two countries will go to war over the town of 12,000 people.

La Bandera de España

Spain's national flag, "La Bandera de España," hasn't been around very long, but that is the case with national flags in general. Most European nations didn't adopt national flags until the era of nation-states began in the 1700s and many didn't do so until the 1800s. Most early national flags were a combination of medieval coats of arms and military flags, which is the case with Spain's national flag.

The earliest iteration of Spain's national flag first flew on Spanish warships in the late 1700s under the rule of King Charles III. The flag features a triband horizontal pattern of a red stripe on the top, a yellow stripe in the middle, and a red stripe on the bottom. The current version of the Spanish flag also features Spain's coat of arms in the gold stripe, slightly off-center to the left. The yellow stripe is twice the width of each of the red stripes.

The coat of arms is a combination of six coats of arms that represent the six major kingdoms that contributed to the formation of modern Spain — Castile, Leon, Aragon, Navarre, Granada, and the

House of Bourbon.

The two crowns represent the King of Spain and the Holy Roman Emperor. King Charles I (remember him?) was not only the King of Spain, but he was also the Holy Roman Emperor, Charles V (1519-1556).

The two pillars represent the strength of the kingdom and the Pillars of Hercules.

Missing from the flag is the Habsburg coat of arms.

As with many national flags, there is some disagreement and even controversy over what the colors represent. It is believed that the colors were chosen because they were those of King Ferdinand II's coat of arms, but not everyone likes to believe in such a mundane origin.

Some believe that the red represents the blood of the Spanish people shed throughout the country's turbulent history, while the yellow either represents the sun or even gold.

That sure makes sense, right?

Others like to think that the colors have to do with bullfighting, the red being the blood of the bulls killed in the arenas, and the yellow representing the arenas' sands. Hmmm, I don't know about that one.

But then again, I'm not Spanish!

Spain's Highest and Lowest Points Aren't on the Mainland

By now, you've learned that Spain has several mountain chains and lowland coastal areas. Many of those mountain chains reach heights of over 10,000 feet and the lowland areas get close to sea level. You might be surprised to learn, however, that Spain's highest and lowest points aren't in Spain proper.

To find Spain's highest point, you'll have to travel to the Canary Islands. If you're ever on the island of Tenerife, you won't be able to miss Pico del Tiede, or "Tiede Peak." Tiede Peak reaches an elevation of 12,198 feet and is a volcano that last erupted in 1909.

Tiede forms the centerpiece of the Teide National Park, which is visited by more than three million people each year.

Since Tiede is an active volcano and since the island of Tenerife is the most populated island in the Canaries with nearly one million people, it poses a significant threat to the population. Because of that, scientists observe the volcano around the clock and there are emergency and evacuation procedures in place should Tiede erupt.

As for Spain's lowest point, it is not some deep canyon or valley, but the Atlantic Ocean, which is off the country's mainland.

Technically, sea level is a mean measurement because it is constantly moving and changing due to the tides, air pressure, and water density. Since, among other factors, the Mediterranean Sea has almost imperceptible tides, the Atlantic wins the contest for the lowest point in Spain.

RANDOM FACTS

1. The city of Almussafes in the Valencian autonomous community is home to the largest Ford manufacturing plant in Europe. The plant produces Fords specifically for the European market, such as the popular Fiesta.

2. The Tagus River is the longest river on the Iberian Peninsula at 645 miles, but it is partially in Portugal. The longest river totally in Spain is the Ebro River, which flows for 578 miles in northeastern Spain.

3. Spain is usually the leading supplier of onions to the rest of Western Europe.

4. Bilbao is the tenth-largest city in Spain, at nearly 350,000 inhabitants and a metro area of over one million. It is the largest city in the autonomous community of Basque Country and is the largest Basque city in the world.

5. The current version of Spain's flag was created in 1978 after the death of Franco. Franco's flag was essentially the same as it is today, but an eagle was perched behind the coat of arms.

6. In October 2017, the people of Catalonia voted for independence in a plebiscite. The Spanish

government declared the vote illegal, which set off the protests and led the president of Catalonia, Charles Puigdemont, to flee Spain as an exile.

7. Mar Menor (Minor Sea), near Cartagena in the southern autonomous community of Murcia, is considered the largest lake in Spain. It is really a salty lagoon that is separated from the Mediterranean by only a thin sandbar. Most of Spain's natural, freshwater lakes are located in the mountainous regions.

8. Spain has a well-developed and maintained highway system and is the third biggest in the world by length. A system of freeways and tollways, known as *autopistas* and *autovias* connect the major cities and every region of the country. If you ever travel on Spanish freeways, just remember that their signs, as in all of Europe, are blue instead of the green used in the United States.

9. Mainland Spain is on the Central European Time Zone, which includes most EU countries. The Canary Islands, though, are ahead an hour, on the Western European Time Zone with the British Isles.

10. The Port of Valencia is the busiest container cargo port in Spain in terms of the number of

containers, while the Port of Algeciras is the busiest in terms of overall volume.

11. Spain has become a leader in alternative/ renewable energy sources in recent years. The country is one of the top European producers of both wind and solar energy and derives more than 40% of its electricity from renewable sources.

12. According to ancient Greek historians and geographers, the Phoenicians were the first people to sail beyond the Pillars of Hercules into the Atlantic Ocean.

13. You might think that the Canary Islands gets its name from the species of bird, but you would be wrong. It came from the Latin word for dog, *"canarie,"* because in ancient times, the island of Gran Canaria was inhabited by large numbers of dogs.

14. The biggest change in Spain's flag took place when the Republicans were in control during the 1930s. They replaced the bottom red stripe with a murrey/purple stripe because they thought the old flag reflected the monarchy too much.

15. Spain is home to two wild feline species, the Iberian lynx and the European wildcat. The Iberian lynx is an endangered species that is only found in scattered parts of southeastern Spain in

the wild. Despite its ferocious-sounding name, the European wildcat is just a wild version of the domestic cat. Unfortunately, although European wildcats may resemble your own Fluffy or Buddy at home, they are impossible to domesticate.

16. Each of Spain's autonomous communities has a flag and president.

17. Gibraltar only has an area of 2.6 square miles. Despite its historical and cultural connections with Spain, the people rejected rejoining Spain in a 2002 plebiscite.

18. If you ever visit Gibraltar, be sure to keep an eye on your possessions, not because of criminals, but because of the thousands of Barbary macaques that roam freely throughout the city. These monkeys' mischievous nature and exotic appeal are a draw for many tourists.

19. Unlike much of the rest of Europe, Spain's borders have remained relatively unchanged for over 100 years, mainly because it was neutral in both world wars.

20. Spain was once home to the Mediterranean monk seal, but it became extinct there decades ago. There have been recent sightings of them in the Balearic Islands, though.

Test Yourself — Questions

1. Which of these colors is not on the flag of Spain?

   a. yellow
   b. blue
   c. red

2. Which mountain range is the border between Spain and France?

   a. Pyrenees
   b. Rockies
   c. Del Sol

3. Barcelona is the capital of which autonomous community?

   a. Catalonia
   b. Basque Country
   c. Galicia

4. Which of these countries does not share a border with Spain?

   a. France
   b. Andorra
   c. Germany

5. The Rock of Gibraltar and Jebel Musa are commonly known as?

   a. The Pillars of Hercules
   b. The Gateway to the Atlantic
   c. The Gateway to Death

Answers

1. b.
2. a.
3. a.
4. c.
5. a.

CHAPTER FOUR:

SPANISH POP CULTURE, SPORTS, ART, AND ENTERTAINMENT INDUSTRY!

Spain is home to a thriving entertainment industry today and has been for several centuries. Did you know that the novel *Don Quixote* was written by a Spaniard and that it was one of the first novels of the modern era? That novel set into motion a process whereby Spain became one of the entertainment and cultural centers not just of Europe, but of the entire world. Other writers and artists, such as Pablo Picasso, followed and left their mark on Spain's cultural landscape.

More recently, Spain has become a hub for film and television, exporting its finished products to Latin America and beyond. Some well-known Spanish actors and actresses have also made the big leap to Hollywood where they have become "A list" stars.

Spain is also known for its traditional music and

dances, many of which are still popular today.

And, of course, you can't talk about Spanish culture without discussing their love of football (soccer). Spain is home to some of the best professional soccer teams in the world, drawing the best players from every continent.

So, get ready to learn about some of Spain's most influential actors, writers, artists, athletes, and more in this chapter.

Spanish Cinema Has an Important and Turbulent History

The Spanish film industry began in the 1890s and by the early 1900s, silent films were being made regularly in Barcelona.

Yes, that's right, Barcelona.

If you remember, Barcelona is Spain's number two city after Madrid, but when it comes to the film industry, it is Spain's Hollywood. Early Spanish silent films were quite popular domestically and many were exported to other European nations and Latin America, making Barcelona a cultural mecca.

But all of that came to an end in the 1930s.

Of course, since you read chapter two of this book, you know that the Spanish Civil War caused chaos in the country and virtually put a halt to many industries. Although the film industry was hurt by the war and most of Spain's silent films were lost in the fighting, both sides employed filmmakers to make propaganda films.

After Franco took over, the government put restrictions on films, requiring that they all be in Spanish, which was a blow to Catalan Barcelona. There were, of course, content restrictions as well. Many filmmakers and actors left the country, but those that stayed found ways around the restrictions and the Spanish film industry survived.

When democracy was restored in the 1970s, there was a renaissance of Spanish cinema, as Spanish films began to be exported again to all corners of the globe, especially Latin America.

One of the more interesting recent trends in Spanish cinema is the production of English language films. These films are produced, written, and directed by Spaniards and often star many Spaniards, but the settings can be anywhere in the world. Some of these films include the 2001 thriller *The Others* starring Nicole Kidman, the 2004 film *Kingdom of Heaven* starring Orlando Bloom, and 2010's *The Way*, which featured Martin Sheen.

So, the next time you're watching a movie, check out the credits—you might be surprised to learn it was produced in Spain.

Conan the Barbarian Was Filmed in Spain

"Conan, what is best in life?"

"To crush your enemies, see them driven before you, and to hear the lamentations of their women!"

If you are a fan of the 1982 sword and sorcery epic, *Conan the Barbarian*, then you are certainly familiar with that line. If you haven't seen the film, it is one of the signature lines spoken by the main character, Conan, played by Arnold Schwarzenegger in his breakout role.

The film is shot in several exotic and diverse locales, ranging from deserts to forests and alpine regions. Although the film overwhelmingly stars Americans, was directed by American John Milius, and was written by American Oliver Stone, it was shot almost entirely in Spain.

Originally scheduled to be shot in Yugoslavia, the film production was moved to Spain due to costs and the possibility of political instability in Yugoslavia. Production headquarters were set up in Madrid, which is also where a set was created.

Alpine scenes were filmed in the northern autonomous community of Castile-Leon and desert scenes were produced in the autonomous community of Andalusia.

The result was a stunning cinematic masterpiece that still wows viewers. Viewers are often surprised to learn that the filming locations featured in *Conan* are in Spain, with many thinking, "Who knew that Spain is so beautiful and has such a diverse landscape?"

Not only did *Conan the Barbarian* help propel Schwarzenegger to stardom—and his eventual, unexpected role as governor of California—it helped establish a precedent for the production of English language films in Spain.

Actress Penelope Cruz Was Born and Raised in Spain

Unless you've been living in a cave for the last 25 years, you've probably seen a film starring Spanish actress Penelope Cruz. Born in 1974, the Madrid native was noticed in her teens for her stunning good looks and her dancing abilities.

It wasn't long before she was cast in music videos, television, and finally, Spanish films.

Because of her fluency in English, Cruz was able to transition to American films in the early 2000s, starring in movies such as the 2001 films *Blow* and *Vanilla Sky, Gothika* in 2003, and 2016's *Zoolander 2*, demonstrating that she has quite an acting range and a wide global appeal.

Now in her forties, Cruz shows no signs of slowing down on the silver screen, which is no doubt helped by the fact that she has retained her unique combination of sex appeal and depth of performance.

Actor Antonio Banderas Is a Native Spaniard

Jose Antonio Dominguez Bandera, better known to audiences around the world as Antonio Banderas, was born in 1960 in the city of Malaga in Andalusia, Spain. Although Banderas now resides in the United Kingdom and has spent much of his life in the United States, he makes sure to keep connected to his homeland, which is where his acting career began in the early 1980s.

Banderas' career began with several small roles in Spanish films that were turned down by other actors who didn't want to be typecast. He played a gay man in the 1987 gay-themed film *La ley del deseo* (*Law of Desire*) and a kidnapper in the 1989 cult hit *Atame!* (*Tie Me Up! Tie Me Down!*). The success of *Tie Me Up! Tie Me Down!* brought him to the attention of Hollywood, and by the early 1990s, he was regularly starring in films. Fast forward to the late 1990s and he was a leading man in "A list" movies such as *The Mask of Zorro*.

All without learning English until he moved to America!

Banderas' lack of English skills is perhaps the greatest part of his story. Since he was the quintessentially tall, dark, and handsome archetype and he demonstrated great range and acting ability in Spain, American producers were quick to hire him. To overcome the language barrier, Banderas memorized his lines phonetically. Eventually, he learned English that way and is now a fluent speaker.

Although Banderas has dialed back his acting roles in recent years, keep an eye out for him in European films. You'll need to pay real close attention because, based on his past roles, he could be playing a wide range of nationalities, personality types, and backgrounds.

The Concept of the Modern Novel Began in Spain

When you're reading *Game of Thrones* or your favorite Tom Clancy novel, have you ever thought about how it began? And by that I mean, not how those particular writers got their ideas, but how the very idea of a novel began. Fictional stories have been around since ancient times, but the idea of the modern novel as we know it began in Spain with Miguel de Cervantes (1547-1616). You may not be familiar with Cervantes' name, but you no doubt have heard of or read his major work—*Don Quixote*.

You know, that story about the crazy guy who attacked windmills!

Well, Cervantes wrote other books and led quite an interesting life; a requirement, of course, for any good novelist.

He was born and lived during the later Renaissance, which allowed him to develop his artistic talents. The exact circumstances that led Cervantes to his literary career, though, remain somewhat of a mystery. He apparently fled Spain due to legal reasons and lived in Rome for several years, where he was surrounded by the art and artists of the Renaissance. It was while he was in Rome that Cervantes began writing and developing the modern novel.

Just like a true starving artist, Cervantes worked an assortment of jobs throughout his life to make ends meet and was involved in numerous interesting adventures.

Cervantes was a sailor in the Spanish Navy. He fought at the Battle of Lepanto (remember that?), was wounded in battle, was later captured by Ottoman pirates, and traveled extensively in a time when people generally never ventured more than a few miles from their homes during a lifetime.

All of Cervantes' adventures provided grist for his novels.

Like many great writers of history, Cervantes became much more famous after he died. Today, he is viewed as one of Spain's greatest heroes and icons.

Spain Has Produced Some Incredible Artists

If you're asked what country has produced the world's best artists, you'll probably answer France or maybe Italy. After all, the Renaissance started in Italy and many of the Modern art movements, such as Impressionism, began in France. But if you dig a little, you'll find that Spain was at the cutting edge of both Renaissance and Modern art.

We already talked about the influence that Cervantes had in literature during the Renaissance, but there were many Spanish painters and sculptors who also left their marks on the world. El Greco (1541-1614) was a true Renaissance man, producing several paintings and sculptures of the highest quality and also establishing himself as a legitimate architect.

Spain also produced some great Renaissance sculptors, such as Gaspar Becerra, and some poets, musicians, and playwrights.

But perhaps Spain's best known and most influential artist was Pablo Picasso (1881-1973).

You're probably familiar with Picasso's unconventional painting style known as "Cubism," which was a Modern art style he developed, but he produced paintings in a wide range of styles long before he became known for Cubism. Picasso's most famous work is titled *Guernica* (1937), which depicts the German bombing of the village of Guernica, Spain during the Spanish Civil War in a cubist style.

In more recent years, Madrid and Barcelona have been home to vibrant art scenes, where artists, writers, and bohemians of all types come to perfect their crafts and—hopefully—to become the next Picasso or Cervantes.

Time for a Nap

We all like to take naps, right? There's something refreshing about laying down for 20 minutes, or even an hour or two, in the middle of the day. It just seems to make things right and get you ready for the rest of the afternoon and the evening. Unfortunately, most of us have jobs or live in countries where taking midday naps during the workweek is impossible, but in Spain, it was once required.

This is called the *siesta*.

If you are familiar with Romance languages, then you can determine that the word "siesta" has to do with the number six. The connection is that it was a traditional nap taken by Spaniards during the afternoon or the sixth hour of the working day. The idea of a siesta was very common throughout most Mediterranean countries, in the Middle East and Europe, but the name comes from Spain. The origins probably come from the Middle Ages when farmers would have big lunches, which—combined with the hot Spanish sun—would make them tired.

So, they started taking two-hour afternoon breaks with a nap.

The Spanish spread the idea to Latin America, where it is still very common in some countries.

Although the siesta may be a tradition in Spain, its popularity has waned in recent years. Spaniards still take two- or three-hour breaks in the afternoon, but they often use the time to run errands or to do non-work related activities.

And don't think that just because Spaniards take long afternoon breaks that they work less. On average, Spaniards work more than most other Europeans; they just work longer into the evening.

As we'll see later, Spaniards are traditionally night owls, so the action doesn't start for them until at least 11:00 p.m. anyway.

You Haven't Danced Till You've Done Flamenco

A beautiful Spanish woman wearing a dress, maybe with a rose in her hair, dancing sensuously to the sound of a guitar: you've probably seen it but didn't know it had a name. There may be vocals accompanying the song and dance, but they aren't necessary.

The dance is what's important.

It's called *flamenco* and it is one of Spain's most recognizable and popular folk dances and styles of music. So popular that more people do flamenco around the world than in Spain itself.

Although no one knows for sure, it is believed by many that flamenco was a music and dance style brought to Spain in the Middle Ages by the Roma/Gypsies, who were originally from India. The style developed in Andalusia, and by the early modern period, it had spread throughout the country.

Watching a flamenco performance might seem a bit strange at first, but it will be less so if you understand some of the important terms. A flamenco song is known as a *cante* and there are generally three types of songs. The *cante jondo*, or "deep song," deals with complex personal issues and is accompanied by more complex guitar music. In contrast, the *cante chico* or "light song," often involves humorous topics. The *cante intermidio*, or "intermediate song,' is a song that mixes elements of the other two songs.

The dance that accompanies a flamenco song, which is the main attraction, is known as the *baile*. The dance was added later in the history of flamenco, and although males and females can do the dance, as well as couples, the female dancers get the most attention. As the dancer taps her feet, twirls her dress, snaps her fingers, and moves her body, she is telling the story with her movements, much as traditional Hindu dancers do in India.

Although it began as a music style of outsiders in Spain, all classes of Spanish society embraced flamenco as their own by the late 1800s and exported it to Latin America. Flamenco became particularly popular in Argentina in the early 20th century.

Now you know what flamenco is, get out there and try it, or at least give it a watch!

Dog Soup Is a Favorite in Andalusia

Yes, you read that right. *Cadillo de perro*, or "dog soup/stew," is a traditional dish in the southern Spanish region of Andalusia. But don't worry, pooches are not used in the production of dog soup, it is just a name.

The soup is a tasty combination of lemons, garlic, and oranges and has an orange color.

So, you're probably thinking, if dog soup is a vegetarian dish, how did it get its name? Well, as much as Spaniards may love dogs, the soup has nothing to do with the animal. According to legend, the soup is named for the nickname of the guy who came up with it.

Spanish cuisine is kind of funny like that. Spanish food is very diverse and changes greatly from region to region. For instance, in the southern regions there is a notable Mediterranean flair.

In the northern region of Asturias, a bean stew is very popular, as are other dishes that are influenced by more northern European and Celtic traditions.

The Basques have a cuisine that includes a lot of fish and lamb dishes; traditionally, the Basques have been either fishermen or shepherds.

Tapas or snacks are popular in all regions of Spain. A tapas is simply a snack or appetizer that can be served cold, usually cheese, bread, or vegetables, or as a cooked *chopito*. A chopito can be anything from small servings of seasoned pork to squid. Tapas are popular in Spain because the Spanish often don't eat their dinner/supper until 10:00 p.m. or later.

Talk about a midnight snack!

Despite the regional differences in cuisine, tapas and pork, in general, tend to be popular throughout Spain.

Sangria and Sherry

If you go to a bar or nightclub in Spain, you'll be able to find many varieties of beer and a host of different liquors, ranging from whiskey to vodka. The two quintessential Spanish alcoholic beverages that are consumed all over the world, however, are sangria and sherry.

Sangria is a dark red wine, which is how it got its name—*sangra* is the Spanish word for "blood." What makes sangria different from other wines around the world, though, is that it is served with chunks of fruit or even orange juice mixed inside it. The chunks of fruit or juice give the wine a sugary—and for many, more palatable—taste. As mentioned earlier in this book, wine production has a long history in Spain going back to ancient times, but it is not known exactly when sangria originated.

By the early 20th century, in addition to within Spain, iced sangria became popular in Puerto Rico, Mexico, and some other Latin American countries, eventually making its way north of the border to the United States.

Spain's other famous alcoholic drink, sherry, is thought of by many as being an English drink since the English enjoy having a sherry during their teatime/happy hour. But the origins of sherry are firmly in Spain during the Middle Ages.

Sherry is a fortified wine made from green grapes. It was originally made in the Jerez, Andalusia, which the Muslims knew as "Sherish," during the early Islamic occupation of Spain. Although the caliphs attempted to restrict alcohol consumption among their subjects, the production of sherry was too good for the economy to outright eliminate.

After the wine is fermented, instead of being bottled, it is put through the distillation process. This is what makes it different from traditional wines. Once the distillation process is completed, it is bottled and aged for three years or more. When you finally sip some sherry, it should have at least a 15% alcohol content.

So, how did sherry become such a popular English drink?

That is quite an interesting story in itself. In 1587, when British privateer/pirate and explorer Francis Drake was plundering Cadiz, he took 3,000 casks of sherry with him. Once the casks were sold on the British market, the English love affair with the Spanish drink began.

You can now get "sherry" that has been produced in several different countries, but they are all imitations. By law, their labels must indicate that they are not true Spanish sherry.

I don't know about you, but I'd rather get a bottle that is marked "sherry" than one that says "Canadian sherry" or "American sherry!"

Bullfighting Was Made Famous in Spain

Many people associate bullfighting with Mexico, but the modern form as it is practiced there came from Spain. In recent years, the popularity of bullfighting in Spain has waned to a certain degree due to

European sensibilities about human—and in this case—animal rights, but many Spaniards continue to support bullfighting as an integral part of their culture.

It is believed that bullfighting can be traced back to ancient Europe and that the first bullrings were gladiator arenas where bulls were hunted and/or used to kill prisoners.

Remember, Spain was part of the Roman Empire.

When the Muslims conquered Spain, bullfighting was almost ended. Many of the caliphs saw it as a pagan celebration and wanted to end it, but it was modified and allowed to continue. Moorish horsemen took part in the events and added their touch to the existing Roman and Visigothic influences.

The place of bullfighting in modern Spanish culture, though, has been seriously questioned by many since the 1980s. Interest in bullfighting remains high with many Spaniards, as evidenced by the reviews of bullfights in Spain's best-selling paper, *El País*. Matadors remain popular and the best are known not only throughout Spain but also in Latin America.

On the other side, though, protests against bullfights have become organized and Catalonia and the Canary Islands have outlawed bullfights.

Some Spaniards fear that the phrase "*torro, torro*" may all but disappear someday, but most believe that there will always be a place for bullfighting in Spain.

The Spanish Call It Fútbol

Americans and Canadians may know the sport as soccer, but in Spain, it is called *fútbol* and without doubt, it is the king of all sports in the land. Football has a long and storied tradition in Spain, first being brought to the country in the 1800s by visiting Englishman and Spaniards who had visited and lived in England, the birthplace of soccer/football.

The first leagues formed in the late 1800s, and by the early 20th century, Spain was becoming known as a football hotbed.

But then the Spanish war happened!

Under the Franco regime, Spanish soccer was somewhat isolated from the rest of the world, as Spain in general was, but after 1975, Spain's national team profile and its professional leagues made great leaps.

Spain hosted the 1982 World Cup, and by the 1990s, the Spanish professional leagues were becoming a top destination for players from around the world. The development of Spanish players and a Spanish style also proved to be successful, culminating with the Spanish national team's win at the 2010 World Cup.

Spain's top professional league is the Liga de Fútbol Profesional, commonly known in English as "La Liga." The most popular La Liga teams are Real Madrid and FC Barcelona and those teams are also intense rivals. Although the rivalry between Madrid and Barcelona has led to violence at times, hooliganism has traditionally not been as nearly as big a problem in Spain as it is in other countries.

The commercial and on-field success of La Liga has led to its teams attracting some of the best talent from around the world, especially other Spanish-speaking countries. Argentine Diego Maradona, Portuguese Cristiano Ronaldo, Argentine Lionel Messi, and—perhaps best known in the English-speaking world—the UK's David Beckham have all played in La Liga.

There is little doubt that La Liga will continue to attract top talent and the Spanish national team will be one of the top teams in the next world cup, ensuring that Spanish football will continue its global impact.

The Basques Have Sports of their own

If you ever have the opportunity to spend time in Basque Country during the summer months, then you'll probably catch what is called *deportes rurales* or Basque rural sports. To an outsider, the games look like part-Scottish Highlander games and part-North American lumberjack games, with stone lifting (*harri jasotzea*), anvil lifting (*ingude altxatzea*), and wood chopping (*aizkora proba*) being three of the more popular events.

Basque rural sports draw large, lively crowds and there is always some betting taking place if you're interested.

The games hearken to a time when the Basques were primarily fishermen, herders, and farmers, so the games reflect those occupations. Winners of the competitions are awarded a beret. Of course, with the Basque Country being part of the modern, Western world, enterprising Basques have taken advantage of the uniqueness of the games by incorporating them into tourist packages.

Just because ETA are communists, doesn't mean that most Basques are!

All that aside, if you do get the opportunity to catch some Basque rural sports, don't expect to see ram fighting or goose pulling.

Yes, I said goose pulling!

Ram fighting was banned in 2007. As for goose pulling, it involved suspending a live goose, or geese head down from a rope. The competitors would then either row out in a boat or ride up on a horse (depending upon if the competition was on sea or land) and attempt to pull the head off the goose while in motion.

Goose pulling was popular outside of Basque Country as well, so don't be too harsh on the Basques. The competition is still played, but thankfully, only dead geese are used now.

Spaniards Love to Gamble

When you look at the numbers, there's no doubt that Spaniards love to take chances with their money. Gambling revenues were more than 13 billion euros in 2017, which was part of a 387% market growth in the industry from 2012 to 2017.

With gambling being legal in Spain, there are plenty of options to chance your money, including casinos, betting houses, and lotteries.

You can play blackjack, roulette, and the slots, or you can go to one of the many betting houses to put a stake on your favorite La Liga side. However, most Spaniards prefer the national lottery, known as *La Gordo* or "The Big One."

The national lottery draw takes place every December 22 and a smaller national lottery, known as *El Nino* ("The Kid"), is drawn every January 5. Spaniards buy shares of the 200-euro price tag of a single ticket for The Big One, believing that it will be worth it since it pays out several million.

And the best part is that Spanish lottery winnings are tax-free!

RANDOM FACTS

1. Victoria Abril was the female lead in *Tie Me Up! Tie Me Down!* She has had a long and successful career in Spain and has starred in a few American films as well, including the 1994 movie *Jimmy Hollywood*, opposite Joe Pesci.

2. Cervantes' *Don Quixote* was published in two parts. The first volume was published in 1605 and the second volume in 1615.

3. To say that Real Madrid and Barcelona are the top two teams in La Liga is no understatement. Real Madrid has won the league's title 33 times and Barcelona 26 times. Now that's dominance!

4. You might be surprised to know that basketball is the second-most popular team sport in Spain. Spain has well-developed amateur and professional leagues and has sent more than a few players to the NBA, including the Gasol brothers, Pau and Marc.

5. Almost as influential in Modern art as Picasso was Salvador Dali (1904-1989), who was born and died in Catalonia. Dali practiced a variety of different art forms but was best known for his surrealist works.

6. Although Spain is famed for its wine and sherry, it also has a long tradition of beer brewing. As is the case in most countries, Spain has a variety of different beers available, with Estrella Damm, Ambar Especial Lager, and Alhambra Especial being three of the most popular.

7. Bullfighting is shown on primetime television in Spain, much to the consternation of some animal rights groups.

8. Maybe even more surprising than basketball's popularity in Spain is the fact that baseball, or béisbol as it is called there, is played in Spain. The sport was brought to Spain by Latin American immigrants, although it has not caught on anywhere near to basketball's level.

9. Julio Iglesias is probably the most recognized Spanish musician in the world. He was born in 1943 in Madrid.

10. Jota is a traditional Spanish song and dance style that originated in Aragon.

11. Approximately one in six adults in Spain is obese, a higher rate than their European counterparts in Italy, France, and Switzerland, but much lower than in Mexico or the USA.

12. Perhaps the best known current Spanish athlete is tennis player Rafael Nadel. He has won 19 grand slam titles and is currently ranked number two in the world.

13. Professional car racing, especially single-seater racing, is a very popular sport in Spain. The biggest racing event in Spain is the Formula One Spanish Grand Prix, which is raced in Montmelo, Barcelona every year.

14. Bullfighter Victor Barrio was gored to death in the ring in the town of Teruel, Aragon in July 2016. Before that, it had been more than 20 years since a bullfighter had been killed in the ring in Spain.

15. The Basques have folk music and dances of their own, with an emphasis on percussion instruments and pipes.

16. Spain is known for many tasty desserts, including crème brûlée, which originated in Catalonia.

17. Matches for the 1982 World Cup were held in stadiums around Spain, but the final between Italy and West Germany was held in the Santiago Bernabéu in Madrid. It is the home stadium of La Liga team Real Madrid and seats more than 80,000 people. Italy won the match 3-1.

18. Juan Ramon Jimenez (1881-1958) was a notable Spanish poet who won the Noble Prize in Literature in 1956. He was known for erotic poems that explored the loss of innocence.

19. The Spanish national soccer team ranks sixth in World Cup appearances with 15. Spain's 2010 victory, though, puts it in elite company as only eight countries have won the coveted title.

20. The Basque game *pelota* became the popular Spanish sport *jai alai*. If you aren't familiar with jai alai, it is sort of like racquetball, where single players, or teams of two, attempt to score points by hitting a ball with a stick of the walls. Betting on jai alai is very popular in Spain. Jai alai was exported to the Americas and is today fairly popular in Florida, especially among the Cuban-American community.

Test Yourself — Questions

1. What is a siesta?

    a. An afternoon nap/break from work
    b. A popular Spanish sport
    c. A popular Spanish drink

2. Of which Spanish city is actress Penelope Cruz a native?

    a. Barcelona
    b. Cadiz
    c. Madrid

3. Which Spanish word does "sangria" come from?

    a. Blood
    b. Water
    c. Wine

4. Which is the most recognizable and globally popular Spanish folk music and dance?

    a. Mariachi
    b. Flamenco
    c. Polka

5. What is the top soccer/football league in Spain?

    a. Premier League
    b. Major League Soccer
    c. La Liga

Answers

1. a.
2. c.
3. a.
4. b.
5. a.

CHAPTER FIVE:

VISTING SPAIN

So, now that you know as much as anybody about Spain's history, geography, and popular culture, it's time to get your plane ticket and plan your trip. In this next chapter, we'll look at some of the best places in Spain to visit. From popular tourist destinations to more out of the way places, Spain offers something for every type of traveler.

If roughing it and backpacking is your thing, there are plenty of options.

There are also many three- and four-star hotels in the country, if you'd rather travel in style.

But, most importantly, no matter who you are, you should never get bored in Spain!

There are plenty of ancient, medieval, and modern historical sites you can visit, lots of great art to check out, and many nightspots to hit.

So, keep reading and learn about some of Spain's best attractions.

Mérida Is a Little Slice of Ancient Rome

If you are traveling in southern Spain through the small autonomous community of Extremadura, then you have to make a stop in Mérida. The city was founded in 25 BC by the first Roman emperor, Augustus Caesar, as a retreat for Roman soldiers, "Augusta Emerita." It then became one of the most important Roman Spanish cities and still bears the distinct façade of its Roman heritage.

Several Roman architectural edifices in Mérida have been well-preserved, which gives the city of about 60,000 charm and a certain amount of authority. A Roman bridge and aqueduct are two utilitarian pieces of architecture to behold, but even more impressive are the remains of the Forum.

Mérida's ancient Forum, which functioned and resembled the Roman Forum, only smaller, is where you can find the Amphitheater and the larger Roman Theater. An ancient racetrack, the remains of a villa, an arch dedicated by Emperor Trajan, temples to the god Mithra and the goddess Diana, baths, and other buildings are also part of ancient Roman Mérida.

Located within the precinct of the ancient Forum is the Museo Nacional de Arte Romano, or National Museum of Roman Art. The museum features Roman artifacts found in and around Mérida and is considered one of the most impressive Roman archaeological museums outside of Italy.

Mérida's Roman heritage is so impressive and historically important that it was dedicated as a UNESCO World Heritage site in 1993.

This Museum Has the Second Largest Collection of Picasso's Works

Barcelona has a lot of sights and things to do, but if you're there and are an art lover, then you need to check out the Museo Picasso or "Picasso Museum." As the name indicates, it is a museum dedicated to the work of Spanish artist Pablo Picasso, with more than 4,000 of his works from all periods of his life. The museum opened in 1963 with a modest donation of Picasso's works by one of his friends and was greatly expanded in 1970 when Picasso donated nearly 1,000 more paintings.

Located in the medieval La Ribera neighborhood in a palace complex, the architecture of the museum is a treasure in itself.

If you aren't a big art aficionado but would like to learn, the Picasso Museum is the perfect place. The paintings are arranged in a more or less chronological order, which will allow you to see how Picasso's art evolved throughout his lifetime. Particularly popular are his "Blue Period" (1901-1904) and "Rose Period"

(1094-1907) paintings, which he did before he took the big leap into Cubism.

You're probably wondering, "If the Picasso Museum in Barcelona has the second largest collection of Picassos, where is the largest?" That would be in Paris, France. Picasso spent much of his life in artist-friendly Paris, but he always remembered his home country.

Those Spanish Royals Sure Collected a Lot of Nice Art

One of the interesting things about royal families throughout history is the way they hoard their wealth. They regularly hide their wealth away in their palaces—even as large segments of their population were poor! This was one of the contributing factors in the French Revolution and also played a role in the Russian Revolution.

The Habsburgs and Bourbons of Spain were no different than other royals of Europe in their hoarding of wealth, but they did it with a bit more style.

They hoarded fine art!

From the Renaissance to the 1800s, the Spanish royals collected some of the best paintings and sculptures in the world, keeping them in their palaces where only they could see them. But after the French royals lost their heads in Spain and a spirit of revolution continued to grip Europe in the 1800s, the Spanish royals began looking at their art horde differently. Finally, in 1819, King Ferdinand VII of Spain, at the behest of this Queen Maria, decided to open the Royal Museum in Madrid to the public. It later became known as the Museo del Prado, or just "the Prado Museum."

If you have the chance to visit the Prado, you're sure to find something you like. Spanish artists such as El Greco and the 19th-century painter Francisco Goya are featured but works from artists all over Europe can also be found there, including Peter Paul Reubens, Raphael, and Henri Matisse, among others.

If the paintings and sculptures in the Prado aren't your type of thing, you can go across the street to the Royal Academy of Arts to check out a rare portrait of American President George Washington (remember, the Spanish helped the Americans in the American War of Independence). Or, if that doesn't interest you, then the Archaeological Museum down the street might. In that museum, you'll find artifacts from the Altamira Cave as well as plenty of Roman objects.

All three museums are located conveniently in central Madrid.

First It Was a Church, Then a Mosque, Then a Church Again

After you've checked out all the great art in the museums of Madrid, it's just a short drive on the A-4 freeway to Cordova (*Córdoba* in Spanish), where you can visit one of the largest and most significant monuments in Spain's history—the Mosque/Cathedral of Córdoba. Located in central Cordova, the mosque is hard to miss because it is part of a large complex that covers several city blocks. It was once the second-largest mosque in the world, only behind the Al-Haram Mosque in Mecca. Today it is a Catholic cathedral, and primarily, a museum.

The Mosque of Córdoba's history began sometime in the 600s CE when the Visigoths used it as a church. It was quite small at the time and only a shadow of what it is today. That all changed when the Islamic ruler Abd al-Rahman I leveled the original structure and had a new, grand mosque built there in 784 CE.

But then that little thing called the Reconquista happened.

The Christians retook Cordova in 1286 and turned the mosque into a church/cathedral, which is what it has remained until the present.

In recent years, the Spanish government has promoted the Mosque of Córdoba as one of the country's top tourist destinations. The campaign has been a major success with more than two million people visiting the Mosque of Córdoba annually.

You can spend an entire day checking out the dozens of chapels and their ornate artwork.

The main attraction, however, is the "Forest of Columns."

The Forest of Columns is a large hall that has 1,300 columns and 760 arches, with a clear influence from both European and Islamic architectural styles.

The mosque/cathedral is open to the public nearly every day and the prices are affordable at 10 euros per adult ticket.

Check Out Spain's Most Controversial Monument

The Valle de los Caídos, or "Valley of the Fallen," is located just outside of Madrid in San Lorenzo de el Escorial. At first, it doesn't seem very controversial. The valley is located beneath a mountain, atop which stands a 500-foot-high cross, which happens to be the largest cross in the world. Below the cross is a Benedictine Abbey and a basilica. In the valley is the monument to the fallen, which holds the remains of more than 40,000 men—Republicans and Nationalists—who perished fighting in the Spanish Civil War.

That all sounds pretty ecumenical and a good way to absolve some of the pain of Spain's past, right? So, where is the controversy? Well, the controversy centers on the fact that it was constructed during Franco's rule and has the dictator's imprints all over it. And, if you remember from earlier, Franco himself was buried there, although his remains will be disinterred sometime soon.

The Valle de los Caídos is about an hour's bus ride from Madrid, shorter if you drive yourself, so it is an easy side trip from the capital city. Besides the more than 300,000 visitors who come there every year to see the giant cross and neo-classical architecture, large numbers of neo-fascists also make pilgrimages there every year on the date of Franco's death, November 20.

Take a Hike!

If you have a little more than a month to spend in Spain and want to get into shape and have a spiritual experience at the same time, consider hiking the Camino de Santiago, often known as the "Way of St. James." The Camino de Santiago is sort of like Europe's version of the Appalachian Trail, just much older and with a religious background.

Beginning in the Pyrenees Mountains, the Camino de Santiago winds 199 miles through some of northern Spain's most beautiful country and ends at the Cathedral of Santiago de Compostela in Santiago, Galicia.

The trail became a popular route for pilgrims from all over Europe during the Middle Ages. They used it to travel to the Cathedral of Santiago, which contains the remains of St. James, believed by Catholics to be holy relics. There are several different paths, but they all end at the Cathedral of Santiago.

If you're planning to hike the entire length, give yourself about 35 to 40 days—rest assured, it will be worth it. You will see medieval churches, beautiful vistas, and will meet plenty of people from around the world along the way. If you schedule things just right, you can see the Running of the Bulls in Pamplona in early July and make it to Santiago in time for St. James Day on July 25.

Whichever path you take, there is a good chance you'll have a profound spiritual experience, as so many have throughout history.

If You're Feeling Daring

If you're feeling daring—and maybe a little crazy—you can head to Pamplona for the Festival of Saint Fermin held every year from July 6-14. You may not have heard of the Festival of Saint Fermin before, but you no doubt have heard about the Running of the Bulls.

The Running of the Bulls is the highpoint of the festival.

So, how does it work?

If you're interested in running with the bulls, you need to be at least 18 years of age, sober, and have a couple of…well, a couple of things that are as big as a bull's!

Basically, you and hundreds of others will be crammed into a street path constructed with temporary fences and then you will run down a nearly 1,000-yard path while being chased by six angry steers into an arena/bull ring.

I'd rather spend my time in Basque Country lounging in a café or hiking in the Pyrenees, but if risking your life in a Hemmingwayesque way is your sort of thing, then have fun.

Every year, there are dozens of injuries, but you may feel good knowing that fatalities are fairly rare. Only one person has died at the event since 2009, and contrary to common perceptions, only one American has died there in the last 100 years.

If You're a Night Owl, You'll Love Spain

If you don't mind taking your evening meals a little later, or a lot later, then you shouldn't have a problem in Spain. As discussed earlier, Spaniards start and end their workdays later than in most other countries, and as a result, often end up taking their evening meal at 10 p.m. or even later.

Some attribute the late meals to the fact that Spain is on a time zone that is ahead of what it should be—Portugal, its Iberian neighbor is one hour behind—while others think it has to do with their laid-back Mediterranean culture.

Either way, if you want to hang out with the locals when you are visiting Spain, be prepared for some late nights and early mornings. No matter if you are in Madrid, Barcelona, Cadiz, or Bilbao, going out at midnight and coming home when the sun is rising is common.

But don't worry, if you get the munchies late at night, you'll have no problem finding a spot that sells some tasty tapas.

Ibiza Is Party Central

If you want to party hard in Spain and be surrounded by just as many Brits as Spaniards while you're doing it, then the Balearic island of Ibiza is the place to be. The small island is located about 90 miles off the Spanish Mediterranean coast on the western edge of the Balearic archipelago. The island has some nice hills and beautiful beaches, but let's face it, if you're going to Ibiza, you're going there to party.

Since the 1970s, Ibiza has been known for its rowdy nightclubs that stay open nearly 24 hours a day.

Nightclubs, pubs, and beachfront bars can be found all over the island of 221 square miles, but most of the bigger and more well-known nightclubs are located in Ibiza Town on the south shore and in San Antoni on the western shore. The nightclubs have attracted professional DJs from around the world that, in turn, have brought many of the world's rich and famous to the shores of Ibiza.

Public drunkenness, fights, and other problems associated with young people being too intoxicated have perturbed many of the locals, so be aware that you are a guest in another country if you visit the island.

The police will not hesitate to bring you to their "motel" if you have too much fun on their island!

Spain Has Sixteen National Parks

If the great outdoors is your thing, then Spain is sure to have something for you in one of its 16 national parks. As described earlier, Spain has quite a diverse topography too, as this is represented well in its parks.

Spain's largest national park is Aigüestortes i Estany de Sant Maurici, which is located in the autonomous community of Catalonia, in the province of Lleida. Situated on the south-central slope of the Pyrenees Mountains, the park encompasses over 100,000 acres of some of Europe's most beautiful land. Mountain peaks in the park reach nearly 10,000 feet, which makes it a favorite among hikers.

The Canaries has the most national parks of any Spanish autonomous community with four. Teide National Park (where Mount Teide is located) is the most popular national park in Spain. Approximately three million of the ten million annual national park visitors in Spain go to Teide to hike up the mountain and view the unique desert landscape.

If you want to see an elusive brown bear or Iberian wolf, then Picos de Europa National Park is the place to go. Located in the Picos Mountain Range of northern Spain in the autonomous communities of Asturias, Cantabria, and Castile and Leon, the Picos National Park was one of Spain's first two national parks created in 1918.

All of Spain's national parks either have modern amenities or have towns and cities nearby, so you won't have to worry about being too far from civilization!

Hit the Slopes

France, Germany, Austria, Italy, and Switzerland may get all the attention and glory for having the best ski resorts in Europe, but Spain has more than a few nice ones for all you skiers. Spain has more than

30 ski resorts located in different regions throughout the country, although most are in the northern autonomous communities.

Baqueira-Beret is the most popular ski resort in Spain. Located on the southern slope of the Pyrenees Mountains in Catalonia, it will cost you about 52 euros to access the resort's nearly 100 miles of slopes. Skiing and snowboarding are both allowed at Baqueira-Beret, which is known for its beauty and the historic charm of its nearby towns and villages.

If you're traveling through southern Spain and want to hit the slopes, don't worry, you still have some options. One of the best resorts in southern Spain is the Sierra Nevada in the autonomous community of Andalusia, near Granada. You can do some intense skiing at the Sierra Nevada during the day and then work your way down the mountain to enjoy the warm Mediterranean at night.

If you're feeling especially adventuresome, you can book a trip with Pyrenees Heliski in Catalonia. The company will fly you to a remote mountain with plenty of powder and then fly you out when you're done.

Some would say that it is skiing the way it was meant to be.

I prefer the lodge and all its amenities!

Madrid's Version of Central Park

After you've visited the museums in central Madrid, if you're tired and just want to relax, head over El Parque del Buen Retiro (Park of the Good Retreat). The park covers over 350 acres, giving Spain's capital city a much-needed green space. Similar to Central Park in New York City, Retiro Park is popular with local and visitors alike and is known for its many wonderful features and attractions.

There is a pond, three art exhibition halls, a rose garden, and a bandstand where you can catch some live music during the summer months. One of the best-known features of the park is the Paseo de las Estatuas (Statue Walk). The Statue Walk features statues of some of Spain's kings that were originally on display in the royal palace during the 18th century.

Since it is a park, there are plenty of bike and walk/running paths available as well.

And just like Central Park, you go for a horse-drawn carriage ride or have your portrait painted by one of the many bohemian artists hanging out in the park.

Girona Is a Relaxing Locale

If you want to get away from the hustle and bustle of Barcelona but want to stay in Catalonia, then make the 60-mile trip up the coast to Girona. This moderately sized city of about 10,000 people has quite a contentious past, changing hands many times between the Christians and Muslims during the Reconquista and being sacked plenty of times in the process.

But that is all in Girona's ancient past.

Today, Girona is known for its moderate temperatures, historic architecture, friendly people, and proximity to Barcelona. It is easy to get to Girona from Barcelona via freeway, bus, or train, and once you're there, you're sure to enjoy your stay.

The city is known for its impressive architecture, especially the medieval Girona Cathedral, construction for which started in the 11th century and was finally completed in the 1800s. The cathedral towers above Girona as a testament to the city's past but also to its present and future. If you're a fan of *Game of Thrones*, you'll notice that the Girona Cathedral served as a set for a season six episode.

If architecture isn't your thing and you want to just relax, there are plenty of cafes and pubs in the city where you can get some sangria and much on some tapas. Many people take side trips to Girona and decide to stay.

Put on Your Dive Suit

To truly see a different side of Spain—or offshore Spain, that is—do some scuba diving in either the Atlantic or Mediterranean. Most tourists come to Spain to see its historical sites, party locations, and national parks, but you'll find another exciting side to the country beneath its waters.

If you're in Barcelona and want to do some excellent Mediterranean diving, you just need to go up the coast a little to the Costa Brava, or "Wild Coast." The region acquired that nickname because of all the rocky cliffs and mountains that jut into the sea, which makes for some great undersea sightseeing!

Also in the Mediterranean, you'll find great scuba diving in the Balearic Islands. If you get tired of partying in Ibiza, you can easily find an affordable yet safe outfitter who will take you scuba diving. The Mediterranean Sea around the Balearic Islands are known for an incredible array of sea life, including eight species of whales and dolphins, so you won't be bored if you go this route.

If you don't want to spend so much on renting a scuba outfit, the Balearic Islands are also known for great snorkeling.

Many people who scuba dive in the Atlantic find the Bay of Biscay a great location, although it has a shorter season due to its colder temperatures.

But the number one Spanish scuba destination for most divers are the waters off of the Canary Islands.

The Canaries are known for their clear, warm water (compared to other locations in the Atlantic) and their diverse range of natural features, including boulders, caves, and swim-throughs. The waters around the Canaries are also home to an incredible amount of marine animal and plant life.

RANDOM FACTS

1. Amnesia Ibiza is one of the biggest and best-known nightclubs on the island of Ibiza. It consistently wins awards for "best club in the world" and can seat (more like stand) 5,000 people.

2. You might be surprised to learn that there is a Guggenheim Museum in Bilbao, Basque Country. Like its American counterpart, the Spanish Guggenheim specializes in Modern art.

3. The Camino Portugués is, as the name indicates, a route to the Cathedral of Santiago that begins in Lisbon, Portugal. It is the only Way of Saint James route that runs in a north-south direction.

4. If you are planning to run with the bulls in Pamplona, be sure to wear the traditional white pants and shirt and red scarf. Many people think that the color red is related to bullfighting and is used to make the bulls angrier, but it isn't. Red is symbolic of the blood Saint Fermin shed when he was martyred in 303 CE.

5. Although Retiro Park may be the best known and most visited park in Madrid, Casa de Campo is by far the biggest park in the city. It is

about five times the size of New York's Central Park, has an amusement park, and is the location of the Madrid Zoo. Unfortunately, though, Casa de Campo is known as a hotbed of sex work and crime, so be careful if you visit.

6. If you're traveling just north of Madrid through the autonomous community of Castile and Leon, you might enjoy a stop in the city of Segovia. Located on a hill over the surrounding plain, Segovia is known for its Roman aqueduct, Gothic cathedral, and medieval castle.

7. If you visit the Sun Coast in Malaga, Andalusia, be warned that many of the beaches are clothing-optional. Millions of Europeans flock to the beaches of the Sun Coast every year to get away from the hustle and bustle of cities such as London and Berlin.

8. Pro-Franco political rallies have been banned by the Spanish government since 2007 and symbols of his regime have been removed from public spaces in Spain. Still, that hasn't stopped his admirers from around the world descending on the Valle de los Caídos every year on his death day.

9. Spain was the second most visited country in the world by tourists in 2018 at 82.8 million visitors. Spain also consistently ranks in the top five best

countries to visit in many different studies and rankings.

10. The Seville April Fair in Seville is the place to go if you want to see flamenco costumes and dance. The festival usually begins about two weeks after Easter.

11. More than 18 million Britons visit Spain every year, by far the number one nationality. The British particularly like the beach towns on the Mediterranean; so much so that some towns resemble British enclaves. The number one non-European nationality to visit Spain is American, with nearly three million Yanks coming to Spain annually.

12. In recent years, Muslims have requested to pray in the Cathedral/Mosque of Córdoba but have been repeatedly denied to do so by the Catholic Church.

13. Terra Mítica is a unique theme park in Benidorm, the autonomous community of Valenciana. The park features traditional amusement park rides, but the park itself is divided into sections by civilization: Egypt, Greece, Rome, Iberia, and the Mediterranean Islands.

14. Spain has 48 locations listed as United Nations Educational, Scientific, and Cultural Organization (UNESCO) World Heritage sites.

15. The Prado Museum gets close to three million visitors per year, making it the 18th most visited museum in the world.

16. The largest collection of Salvador Dali's works is housed in the Dali Museum in Figueres, Catalonia. The museum usually gets over one million visitors annually and is only about 25 miles from Spain.

17. The most visited museum in Spain is the Museo Nacional Centro de Arte Reina Sofía, or "El Reina" in Madrid. It is a museum of 20th-century art, so you'll find some works by Picasso, but also lesser-known Spanish artists from the period. It had nearly four million visitors in 2018.

18. In case you're wondering, the legal drinking age in Spain is 18, but in the autonomous community of Asturias, it's 16.

19. If you want to smoke some pot while you're in Spain, you should be aware of the somewhat tricky laws. It is illegal to sell marijuana and a misdemeanor to possess it in public, but it is legal to consume and possess it for your personal use.

20. Crime in Spain is generally low and on par with the rest of Europe. The overall rate is much lower than the United States, with only 364 homicides in the entire country in 2012, but there

are some things you need to be aware of when traveling there. Tourists are often targeted for pickpocketing and hotel burglaries, so be aware and try not to look like a mark!

Test Yourself — Questions

1. Spain's centuries-old, world-famous hiking trail is known as the?

   a. Carmen San Diego
   b. Camino Real
   c. Camino de Santiago

2. Where are more than 40,000 men who died fighting on both sides of the Spanish Civil War buried?

   a. Tomb of the Unknown Solider
   b. Valley of the Fallen
   c. Madrid National Cemetery

3. What is the largest national park in Spain?

   a. Basque Country National Park
   b. Aigüestortes i Estany de Sant Maurici National Park
   c. Barcelona Shores National Park

4. Which Spanish ski resort do ski bums like the best?

   a. Baqueira-Beret
   b. Balaclava Hills
   c. Veil

5. Which island is party central for many Europeans?

   a. Tenerife
   b. Menorca
   c. Ibiza

Answers

1. c.
2. b.
3. b.
4. a.
5. c.

CHAPTER SIX:

WEIRD SPAIN—LEGENDS, GHOST STORIES, AND THE STRANGE!

You might not think of Spain as a country with a "weird" past or present, but there are plenty of strange and fascinating stories circulating throughout it. Some of them are based on history, while others seem to have no basis in reality at all.

In this chapter, you'll learn about a legendary lover whose name you are familiar with and a legendary knight who really lived but was later made into a national hero. Some of the strange details and origins of Spanish folk and religious festivals will also be explored.

But it really wouldn't a chapter about the weird without some ghost and monster stories, would it?

You'll be introduced to a couple of ghost stories that are sure to make you shiver and a couple of urban myths that prove people around the world often have more in common than we think. So, keep reading and be prepared to be very fascinated and maybe just a little creeped out!

El Cid Is Spain's National Folk Hero

Without a doubt, Spain's favorite son and national hero was an 11th-century knight named Rodrigo Diaz de Vivar, or more popularly, "El Cid." In many ways, El Cid is the King Arthur of Spanish folklore— he was a historic personality, but his exploits have been exaggerated over the centuries to reach legendary status. El Cid's exploits were recorded in the semi-fictional *The Poem of the Cid* in the 12th century and the rest, as they say, was history.

So who was El Cid and why is his legend so important in Spain?

El Cid was a noble from Castile who lived during the tumultuous period of the Reconquista. He originally fought for the Christians against the Muslims, gaining great fame for his bravery and battlefield tactics, earning the respect of both sides.

So much respect, that the Muslims began calling him El Cid, which was probably a Spanish-Arabic form of "master."

But with great success often comes jealousy and intrigue, which led to El Cid being exiled from Castle.

With nowhere to turn, the enterprising commander did as many his situation throughout history have done—he offered his services to his former enemy.

Alfonso VI of Castile eventually realized his mistake and lifted El Cid's exile, but by that point, Rodrigo had ambitions and an army of his own.

El Cid used an army of Spanish and Moors to conquer Valencia, ruling the city on behalf of Alfonso VI. The Muslims eventually sieged and captured Valencia, killing El Cid in the process. That is where the legend gets really good.

One variation of the legend states that El Cid's wife, Jimena, dressed his corpse in his suit of armor, placed it on his horse, and paraded it in front of the troops to build their morale. If that happened, it didn't work, because the Muslims retook the city.

El Cid and his wife were interred in the Burgos Cathedral, where they remain to the present.

The legend of El Cid has inspired books, movies, and even video games in the modern era, but for the Spanish, it represents qualities that they all seek to emulate, such as chivalry, honesty, loyalty, wisdom, intelligence, and tenacity.

The Cursed Metro Station

If you happen to catch the metro (subway) in Barcelona, be aware if you're on the Red Line. On that line is a station that the locals and metro workers often try to avoid. The Rocafort station lies beneath the Eixample district of Barcelona, just outside the old city.

What is of interest here, though, isn't what's happening on the streets, but what's taking place below in the Rocafort metro station. You see, according to employees of the Barcelona metro, not only is the station haunted, but it also seems to be cursed.

Since the Barcelona metro doesn't run 24 hours a day, all stations close for cleaning and maintenance between 11:00 p.m. and 2:00 a.m., which is when employees at the Rocafort station have reported seeing and hearing strange things.

Some have even claimed that cameras have picked up some bizarre images.

Many of these reports can and have been explained as a combination of boredom and overactive imaginations, but that can't explain away the abnormally high number of suicides at the station. There were even four in one month!

A quest to find answers uncovered that the location served as a sanctuary during the Spanish Civil War, which was immediately cited as the reason for the alleged curse.

Could the Rocafort metro station be haunted by the ghosts of Republican refugees?

Make a trip there and decide for yourself.

If You're Bad, El Coco Will Get You

If you're from the English-speaking world, as a kid you were probably told at some point that if you weren't good, the Boogieman would get you. The chances are that you weren't given many details about what the Boogieman looks like or what his M.O. is, other than that he hides under beds.

Spain's version, El Coco, "The Skull," is a much more graphic take on the legend. According to the Spanish legend, El Coco whisks away disobedient children and then drinks their blood and eats them.

Anthropologists and historians cannot say for sure when or how the story began, but many believe it was part of Iberia's pre-Christian history, as the legend is shared with Portugal. El Coco was also associated with a dragon in Iberia's early Christian history, but it was a real event in the early 20th century that brought the El Coco story to life.

In 1910, a man from the town of Gador named Francisco Ortega was diagnosed with tuberculous. In those days, a TB diagnosis could be fatal; at the very least it meant a much shorter, painful life.

Ortega was desperate for a cure.

He visited a local faith healer named Agustina Rodriguez, who enlisted the help of her barber friend, Francisco Leona. Rodriguez told Ortega that the blood and fat of a child would cure him of his ailment, so a 7-year-old boy named Bernardo Parra was kidnapped off the streets as a prescription.

Ortega paid the healer and dutifully drank the helpless boy's blood and rubbed some of his fat over his body as prescribed. Needless to say, the conspiracy was soon uncovered by the authorities and the main perpetrators were quickly executed.

Ortega's TB was cured at the end of a rope!

Sometimes, people make the scariest monsters of all.

The Vampire of Barcelona

By all accounts, Enriqueta Martí was a woman who lived on the fringes of society. Born 1868 in a small town, Martí moved to the big city of Barcelona to be a maid, but after earning only just enough to get by, she found out that it paid more to sell her body. Martí soon found that her good looks were in demand, but she also knew that sex work wasn't something she could do for very long.

So she decided to go into business for herself.

Martí opened a brothel that catered to the Barcelona's elite and their more "eclectic" sexual tastes. To meet the demand of her new client base, Martí went to the lower class neighborhoods to find unsuspecting children, whom she enticed by offering food, candy, and toys.

But this is only the beginning of this very twisted story.

Martí was also a witch doctor who believed that the blood and fat of children could cure a variety of different diseases (sound familiar?). So, if the police began searching for one the children Martí had abducted, she simply murdered him or her and then used the kid in one of her brutal rituals.

No body, no evidence, right?

Well, not exactly. In 1912, she abducted a poor girl named Teresita Guitart Congost, but unlike all the other children before her, the police took an interest in her disappearance. Eventually, the police ended up at Martí's brothel where they found Congost and another girl, still alive. They also found several bones and bone fragments of children, along with some blood-covered items.

Martí was promptly arrested and charged with murder, but she never made it to trial; her fellow inmates murdered her in the city jail on March 12, 1913.

Many believe that Martí's murder was orchestrated by Barcelona's elite, who were afraid that their unnatural deeds would become public at trial. Others suggest that some of the women who killed Martí were in fact mothers of her victims. Many questions remain about the Vampire of Barcelona, including her precise body count, although it is believed to be at least 20 and probably more, making her one of the most prolific female serial killers in history.

If you're walking down Carrer de Joaquín Costa in the Raval neighborhood, listen real closely when you get to #29. You might hear the ghosts of some of Martí's victims or you might even hear the shriek of the Vampire of Barcelona herself!

Don Juan Is a Spanish Legend

No doubt you've heard and probably used the term "Don Juan" at some point in your life. The name usually refers to a ladies' man and often a womanizer, with it having either a positive or negative connotation depending on the person and the context.

Originally, the term had quite a negative connotation.

Unlike El Cid, who was based on a historical person, Don Juan is a purely fictional character created during Spain's golden age in the 17th century. If you aren't familiar with the general story, it is about a Spanish noble named Don Juan who spends all of his time seducing women through a variety of ruses, often in disguise. Most versions of the story end in tragedy, with Don Juan being sent to hell for sins ranging from adultery to murder. There have been several different versions of Don Juan since the 17th century, but they all share common themes—Don Juan is the archetype of a shallow, amoral, and rapacious individual.

In the end, Don Juan always gets what's coming to him.

So, the next time you are one of your friends aspires to be a "Don Juan," remember that things didn't end well for the legendary Spanish lover.

La Chica de al Curva

The legend of the mysterious hitchhiker has appeared in many different countries in recent decades. The stories go that, if you are driving at night along a certain road, at a certain time, you might find a disturbed looking young woman walking alongside the road. The ending varies from place to place—sometimes she is dropped off at a cemetery where the driver finds her tombstone after she mysteriously vanishes, or she is brought to her former residence where she disappears.

The Spanish legend follows a similar formula. If you are driving alone on a lonely two-lane highway, usually in a hilly or mountainous region, be wary of picking up a young female hitchhiker on the road. If you do, the girl will make small talk with you before quickly ending the conversation to warn you about a deadly curve coming up in the road.

After avoiding the curve and turning to thank your passenger, you'll notice that she has miraculously disappeared!

People throughout Spain still report this supernatural phenomenon, so if you're in Spain and driving alone at night in a rural, mountainous area, watch out for those curves.

The Winds of La Mancha

When you're in the southern half of the Castilla-La Mancha autonomous community, in the region known as La Mancha proper, listen very closely to the wind. You see, La Mancha is known for its strong winds, which power the many medieval-style windmills you'll see dotted across its landscape. However, many people also claim to hear other sounds within those winds.

La Mancha has been long-known as a hotspot of paranormal activity, where ghosts are routinely heard and seen. One place in La Mancha that seems to be a particular magnet for ghosts, poltergeists, and other visitors from the beyond is the University of Castilla-La Mancha in Ciudad Real.

The university itself was established in 1982, so most of the buildings are relatively new and spook free, but the office of the president is much older and once served as a shelter that was run by nuns. There have been numerous reports of spectral activity in the president's office, ranging from doors opening and closing, seemingly by themselves, to sightings of shadow-like apparitions.

Skeptics dismiss the activity at the university as a combination of overactive imaginations and the fabled winds of La Mancha. But not everyone is so quick to write off a possible otherworldly explanation for the scary activity at the University of Castilla-La Mancha.

It seems the only way to know for sure may be to take a trip there yourself.

A Dead Species Reborn?

Remember way back in Chapter 3 when we discussed some of Spain's native animals? One of those species, the Pyrenean ibex, became extinct in 2000. The loss left biologists and conservations frustrated, but a group of geneticists came up with a revolutionary answer to the loss—create a clone. In 1996, the first mammal had been successfully cloned when Dolly was "created" in England, so scientists in Spain thought it was wise to take a tissue sample from the last known living Pyrenean ibex, Celia, in 1999.

Two teams of Spanish scientists and a team of French scientists then set about working out how to grow a Pyrenean ibex cell and the fetus inside the body of another animal species.

In a complex process known as nuclear transfer cloning, the cells from Celia were placed inside a goat's eggs, with the goat DNA being removed.

The extremely difficult and complex experiment yielded no viable fetuses until July 30, 2003, when a clone of Celia was born. Although the clone died not long after being born due to an extra lobe in the lung, it was a tremendous step in genetics and biology. The Pyrenean ibex technically became the first "unextinct" animal species in world history and the knowledge of cloning techniques was greatly advanced.

There's no telling what will come next in the field of cloning or if another attempt to revive the Pyrenean ibex will be successful, but there's a good chance it will happen in Spain.

A Moorish Romeo and Juliet

Spanish folk tales so often involve heroic figures who are lovers as much as they are fighters. Most of these folk tale characters' lives end in a tragedy, which I guess is part of the reason why these are timeless tales. Perhaps the most tragic of all Spanish folk tales involves a Moorish family known as the Abencerrages.

According to the legend, the Abencerrages was a Muslim family that probably came to Spain not long after the Islamic conquest in the 8th century. The family lived in the Kingdom of Granada and by the 15th century had become very influential and wealthy.

But with wealth and power comes jealously and enemies.

The equally wealthy and influential Moorish Benedin family despised the Abencerrages family and would do anything to best them, or better yet, to destroy them.

The opportunity came for the Benedin family when they learned that the head of the Abencerrages family was involved in an illicit affair with the Sultan of Granada's favorite concubine. Some versions of the legend say that a Benedin family member told the sultan, while other versions say the sultan learned another way. Either way, the sultan was not happy.

The sultan invited most of the adult members of the Abencerrages family to dine in a sumptuous hall of the Alhambra Castle. When the Abencerrages family members arrived, the doors to the hall were locked and they were promptly sliced and diced by the sultan's henchmen.

It is said that the slaughter was so great that a

permanent bloodstain was left on the bottom of the fountain in the hall. Perhaps the most tragic part is that the sultan was the last Islamic ruler in Spain; if the Abencerrages family could've just waited a little longer, they would've lived!

The dining hall where the slaughter supposedly took place was renamed the Hall of the Abencerrages. Although most historians argue that the lack of textual evidence of the massacre means that it probably didn't happen, locals are positive that it did and point to the red stain in the fountain as proof.

Others claim that they've heard faint voices pleading for mercy in Arabic in the hall.

The Creepiest Haunting in Madrid's History

In early 1990, Estefania Gutierrez Lazaro was like most teenage girls. She liked boys and spending time with her friends and family, but she did have one interest that set her a little apart from other young adults—she had a deep interest in the occult.

Estefania and her friends liked to perform séances and play with Ouija boards in attempts to contact dead. According to her parents, the young woman's interest in the occult led to her death and a creepy supernatural experience that was witnessed by several people.

The Lazaro family led a quiet, middle-class life in the Vallecas neighborhood of Madrid. Their children were well-behaved, including Estefania, although she was a little bit secretive.

It is believed that things got really creepy when Estefania and some of her friends were playing with a Ouija board at school. A nun caught them and made them stop. As the girls were preparing to leave their make-shift séance, they reported seeing a cloud of smoke emanate that then seemed to go inside Estefania.

From that point on, things went downhill for the young woman.

Estefania claimed to see large shadow figures throughout the family's home and, as her mental condition deteriorated, so too did her physical condition. By the summer of 1991, Estefania had become so sick that her parents had her hospitalized, but it was too late; she died of an apparent heart attack in the hospital.

Looking for answers for their daughter's seemingly unnatural death, the Lazaros did some detective work and found out about Estefania's fascination with the occult.

Then things changed for them as well!

The Lazaros began seeing tall, shadowy figures throughout their home, along with several other unexplainable occurrences ranging furniture moving at will to voices coming from the empty bathroom. Finally, in early 1992, it became too much for the family when Mrs. Lazaro woke in the middle of the night to what felt like someone sitting on top of her.

They called the Madrid police for assistance.

The police were quickly introduced to the phenomenon, hearing loud noises with no accompanying action and seeing doors open on their own. The creepiest things happened when they went to Estefania's bedroom. As the police looked around the room, a crucifix turned upside down and a poster was ripped to shreds, apparently by an invisible force, right before their eyes. And to top it all off, a framed picture of Estefania fell off the wall and caught fire but didn't burn anything around it.

It was too much for some of the officers, who ran from the home never to return.

It was also apparently too much for the Lazaro family because they moved to another home, and luckily for them, whatever it was didn't follow them.

If you have the nerve, check out the fictional portrayal of the events in the 2017 film *Veronica*. But trust me, don't watch it alone!

Franco's Mystic Advisor

Like all military strongmen, dictators, and fascist leaders, Francisco Franco presented a carefully crafted image to the Spanish public. Almost always dressed in a nicely pressed military uniform with plenty of medals, Franco appeared calm and in control when he made public appearances, a true *caudillo* with an iron will.

But beneath the façade, Franco had some insecurities and bizarre behaviors, one of which was frequenting a mystic.

The mystic Franco regularly consulted was a Catalonian nun named Ramona María del Remedio Llimargas Soler. After Soler predicted the Spanish Civil War, her reputation as a seeress became widely known in Spain, so Franco decided to elicit her services.

Soler supposedly prevented Franco from being assassinated and advised him at the Battle of Ebro in November 1938, which proved to be the final blow against the Republican army.

Soler, who Franco referred to as "Ramona the Catalan," also told Franco which of his inner circle were Free Masons, so he could promptly have them arrested as part of his anti-Mason crusade.

Sister Romana died in 1940, leaving behind somewhat of a mixed legacy. Although she supported Franco, she is also believed to have helped the Republicans, possibly acting as a spy. She believed in order and, like most Catholics at the time, saw Franco's anti-Mason campaign as righteous, which played a major role in her helping the dictator.

Whatever Sister Romana's reasons for helping Franco, their ties are certainly a strange footnote to the dictator's life.

Are They Really Wearing That?

If you ever visit Seville the week before Easter, you'll see plenty of excitement throughout the country. If you're an American, you'll probably pause when you notice a bunch of people wearing what appear to be Ku Klux Klan robes!

Rest easy; the festival of La Candelaria had been taking place long before America was even a country, so it has nothing to do with race, politics, or anything at all related to the pro-segregation organization. So, why do people wear those robes and what is the festival all about?

Well, the hooded figures—many of them children—are part of parade marchers who carry out renditions of scenes, known as *pasos*, which depict the events from Jesus' crucifixion. Only members of a confraternity of penance are allowed to wear the hood, known as a *capirote*, in the processions. Those marching in the processions often carry candles, which is how the festival got its name.

The hood originated in the Middle Ages during the Spanish Inquisition and was used as a form of punishment. The use of the hood eventually evolved to symbolize that the person wearing it was a member of the Brotherhood of La Candelaria and that he was doing public penance for his sins.

So, as strange as the outfits of the La Candelaria Brotherhood may look, they have nothing to do with the KKK.

The Greatest and Most Cursed Opera House in Spain

On April 4, 1837, the Gran Teatre del Liceu, or just the "Liceu," opened in Barcelona as Spain's premier opera house. In the time since the Liceu opened, some of Europe's top actors and opera singers have graced its stage, bringing some of the greatest tragedies ever written to the Spanish people.

But the Liceu has also been the location of several real-life tragedies.

Like so much of Spain's history, the Liceu's past mixes true history with legend and begins in the contentious period of the Reconquista. Many of the legends state that the location where the Liceu was built was used as a torture and execution ground during the Middle Ages. It was utilized by both Christians and Muslims, depending upon who controlled Barcelona at the time. Many believe that the ground's early bloody history left the Liceu with a curse that it will never be able to shake.

The first tragedy struck on April 9, 1861, when a fire engulfed much of the building. But the owners of the Liceu pooled their resources and hired some of the best architects and workers to rebuild the theater. Exactly one year later, the Liceu reopened for business.

An even worse tragedy struck the Liceu on November 7, 1893, when an anarchist named Santiago Salvador hurled two bombs into the crowd, killing 20 people and injuring many more. Salvador thought he would strike a blow against the bourgeoises by destroying one of their theaters, but the Liceu was only closed for about two months.

The Liceu survived the Spanish Civil War and even began thriving in the decades from World War II until the 1990s. Attendance was high and so were the profits, with top talent coming from around the world to perform in the hall.

Then, on January 31, 1994, another fire consumed the Liceu. The theater was closed for five years after the fire, although no major tragedies have hit the theater since.

Many people laugh at the idea of the Liceu being cursed, labeling it pure superstition. They argue that everything that happened there was purely coincidence and that no major tragedies have hit the theater in twenty-five years. Those who believe the Liceu is cursed say that there were often long periods between tragedies and that, most importantly, there is no such thing as a coincidence!

RANDOM FACTS

1. Alhambra Castle was built in 889 CE on the remains of an ancient Roman fortress. The Hall of the Abencerrajes is a perfect square with a dome, following typical Moorish architecture.

2. You may think that the legend of St. George and the Dragon is a purely English tale, but the Spanish have another version: "San Jorge y el Dragon." The Spanish version is celebrated every April 23 in Barcelona.

3. On November 11, 1979, a commercial jet flying over Ibiza had to make an emergency landing in Valencia after a mysterious set of red lights followed the plane. The Spanish government later said that lights were a reflection from a nearby chemical factory, but the crew and 109 passengers of the flight weren't so convinced by that explanation.

4. American actor Charlton Heston is perhaps the best-known person to portray El Cid. He did so in the 1961 film *El Cid*.

5. The earliest known depiction of Don Juan was the ca. 1630 play, *The Trickster of Seville and the*

Stone Guest by Gabriel Tellez. Don Juan is murdered at the end of the play for his numerous transgressions.

6. Because she supported Franco, Sister Ramona is somewhat of a controversial figure in modern Spain. Although nuns typically support the poor, many of the more radical members of the Republicans were anti-Catholic, while the Nationalists were pro-Catholic. She claimed to not be political, which is perhaps demonstrated by her support of both sides, if only slightly, during the war.

7. Carrer 20 Jose Torres in Barcelona is worth a look if you get the chance. It is adorned with demon sculptures and statues because, according to the legend, one of the former owners made a deal with the devil to become rich in this life. After making lots of money, the man decided to pay homage to the Dark Lord by adorning the house with creepy sculptures.

8. Celia, the last Pyrenean ibex, was killed by a broken branch. Although cloning is possible and a way to bring the Pyrenean ibex back, the problem is that there would only be females of the species.

9. Besides the woman on the curvy road, Spain has some other urban legends that are known in other countries, including the story that giant alligators that live in the Madrid sewer system.

10. Many people believe that the Reina Museum in Madrid is haunted. People have claimed to have seen and heard many strange things there over the years. It turns out that the building that now houses the museum was once a hospital — so maybe they have!

11. The Spanish term for a faith healer is *"curandero"* (male) or *"curandera"* (female). Unlike the two cases profiled in this chapter, most Spanish faith healers have traditionally used legal — although medically questionable — prescriptions for their clients. Curanderos are not very common today in Spain, but they still are in many parts of Latin America.

12. Although curanderos have fallen in popularity in Spain, more than half of all Spaniards use homeopathic remedies.

13. You might find this hard to believe, but Spain has a version of Bigfoot. For years, there have been reports of a big, hairy hominid, called "Basajaun," roaming the hills and mountains of Basque Country. The people of the region

haven't yet cashed in on the sightings with any merchandise.

14. The number 13 is universally considered an unlucky number, but in Spain Tuesday the 13th is the unluckiest of all days, not Friday the 13th.

15. During the Inquisition, the *capirote* was made from paper, but today it is made of fabric and usually has the symbol of the wearer's particular brotherhood stitched onto it.

16. Retiro Park has a very bizarre claim that makes it unique among all other places—it is the only place in the world with a statue of the Devil. The statue, called *The Fallen Angel*, was made by Ricardo Bellver in 1922 as an homage to John Milton's *Paradise Lost*.

17. The Spanish take their drinking and toasting very seriously, so make sure to make eye contact with everyone in the toast. Whatever you do, don't toast with a glass of water. They say you'll be cursed with seven years of bad sex!

18. If you get a room in the Cardona Castle/hotel just outside of Barcelona, don't ask for room 712. It is supposedly very haunted and is off-limits to both guests and staff.

19. While in many countries the color red is

associated with the devil, evil, and hell, in Spain it is yellow.

20. If you're a cat lover, be aware that in Spain, Fluffy only has seven lives. It's unknown where she lost the other two, as Spain has its fair share of cat lovers, but for whatever reason, cats need to be a little more careful in España.

Test Yourself — Questions

1. Which extinct animal was successfully (sort of) cloned in Spain?

    a. Pyrenean brown bear
    b. Iberian wolf
    c. Pyrenean ibex

2. Which of these is not a legendary Spanish character?

    a. El Cid
    b. Don Juan
    c. Casanova

3. Which Barcelona theater has been plagued by many tragedies?

    a. Liceu
    b. Savoy
    c. Orpheum

4. Which of these is the Spanish version of the Boogieman?

    a. Caudillo
    b. El Coco
    c. El Taco

5. What is the name of the metro station in Barcelona that many think is cursed?

    a. Rocafort
    b. Union Station
    c. Don Juan Centro

Answers

1. c.
2. c.
3. a.
4. b.
5. a.

DON'T FORGET YOUR FREE BOOKS

GET THEM FOR FREE ON
WWW.TRIVIABILL.COM

I hope you enjoyed this book and learned something new. Please feel free to check out some of my previous books on <u>Amazon.</u>